FOREWORD

We live in a *disintegrating* society. This is not a gloomy prognostication of incipient breakdown, but simply means that the proliferation of detail involves an increasing departure from unity and is thereby an exercise of a *decreasing* consciousness. Real progress entails a response to the integrating influences in the Universe, but this is only vaguely understood in the hypnotism of material achievement.

Such was my own experience. I was trained as a scientist and for many years was fully and happily occupied with the exciting activities of my profession. I paid lip-service to conventional religious beliefs, which I regarded as relevant to a vaguely-defined future existence. In middle life, however, a chance encounter brought me into contact with the late Maurice Nicoll, whose philosophy provided me with entirely new horizons.

I discovered that science and religion are not incompatible, but are complementary aspects of a Universe of far greater magnificence that I had formerly envisaged, and which gradually began to acquire for me a living reality. The process involves a kind of psychological alchemy by which the everyday experiences of life are transformed in quality. They become part of a more meaningful pattern of which one is aware *simultaneously* with the necessary life activities. How this may be achieved in practice I have endeavoured to illustrate from my own experience.

J. H. Reyner

CONTENTS

FIGURES

CHAPTER ONE

THE REAL ADVENTURE

"Where shall I begin, please your Majesty?" asks the White Rabbit in Lewis Carroll's immortal classic. "Begin at the beginning", says the King gravely, "and go on till you come to the end; then stop." Life, though, has many beginnings and endings. It is a succession of experiences, some trivial, others more meaningful, each of which in its time occupies our attention and interest. When we are very young, every day is a new adventure, but this sense of delight is soon subordinated to the apparently more significant pursuit of attainment.

One's early life, indeed, is necessarily occupied with learning how to contend with the conditions of existence. We find ourselves in a world which in many respects conforms to recognisable and consistent laws, but in which the pattern of events seems to be at the mercy of an arbitrary, and even capricious, Fate. For us, meaning is derived primarily from pitting one's wits against the vagaries of chance, which becomes an absorbing, and often exciting exercise affording little opportunity for speculation as to any deeper implications.

There are some who believe that this is, in fact, the only meaning in life. They maintain that man has no individual destiny, his usefulness being determined solely by the contributions he makes to the fund of human knowledge. Yet most of us are not entirely convinced by these assumptions of human omni-science and acknowledge an innate, if inarticulate, belief in an Intelligence of a superior order. We are content to regard life as a kind of proving ground, in which the kaleidoscopic, and often apparently unjust, experiences constitute some form of preparation for a future state of existence.

Such was the comfortable philosophy of my youth, based on an uncritical acceptance of a conventional religious upbringing. It makes no demands beyond conformity to an idealistic code of morality, within which one is free to pursue the ambitions of material comfort and success to the best of one's ability. These activities provide a satisfactory, and even exciting meaning. Yet after a time a certain staleness creeps in. Every achievement merely creates the desire for more. We attempt to vary the pattern by seeking new experiences and relaxations, or even by changing our environment; but the escape is illusory, for we find that the new situations are basically 'the mixture as before'. Gradually we begin to perceive that the only real adventure is that of life itself.

This, however, seems to be in the nature of a mystery tour. By the rules of the game we are only aware of the immediate scene, so that the overall pattern and the ultimate destination remain obscure. The adventure is even more curious in that it is not a journey in chronological time, but involves an expanded awareness of all one's experience; and this we find difficult to understand because all our ordinary attitudes regard development as necessarily taking place in the future.

There are individuals who, perhaps having made the tour before, have a clearer idea of where they are going, but for ordinary mortals like myself the essence of the adventure lies in the discovery for oneself of this greater awareness; and it proves to be a remarkably inspiring exercise.

*   *   *

If one seeks beginnings, it seems that my career really started during an English lesson at school when the master quoted the aphorism 'Take your opportunities, or make them'. This appealed to my youthful enthusiasm as a commendably practical maxim, which became the rule and guide of my faith. Its immediate impact was to create a certain irresponsibility of character which was to cause me much trouble later, and my school life was undistinguished.

Nevertheless, by a combination of diligence and fortune I obtained a scholarship to the City & Guilds Engineering College, from which I graduated in my early twenties and joined the newly-formed Radio Section of the Post Office. The work was intriguing, for the art was in its infancy; but even more exciting prospects were opened up by the birth of broadcasting, creating a growing army of enthusiastic amateurs who constructed their own receivers from designs published in a variety of popular journals.

In 1925 a tempting opportunity arose to join one of these organisations and I decided to forsake the security of Government service for the more adventurous field of radio journalism. Here I immediately found my métier, for I was able to combine a natural inventiveness with a flair for writing which began to bring me a certain reputation. The easy days of the home-constructor era did not last, but by that time I was sufficiently established to set up as an independent consultant and later to form my own manufacturing organisation, which provided an adequate and exciting living.

It was a period of rich adventure, including a happy family life and a variety of recreational interests such as flying. The details are unimportant because all this activity was no more than the necessary, but mechanical, accumulation of life experience which we each have to undertake in our own particular sphere.

In general, this phase of one's life is governed mainly (and quite rightly) by personal ambition. Yet there are occasions when one is aware of a certain element of destiny. We all experience chance encounters, and even apparent misfortunes, which affect the whole course of our lives. I became a radio engineer by accident, for it was not my intention at college, where it was regarded as a second-rate pursuit. Yet it was a field of pristine opportunities particularly appropriate to my latent talents, for which I often felt a sense of gratitude. There have been many such 'accidents' in my life.

Celtic legend attributes such experiences to Queen Mab, the fairies' midwife who brings to birth men's secret hopes while they sleep. There is a similar suggestion in Hamlet's dictum, 'There's a divinity that shapes our ends, rough-hew them how we will'. I have always found this an inspiring idea, not in the sense of some grim pre-destination, and still less in the belief that one's life is personally and individually directed by a benevolent Diety, but as an indication that life contains certain (unsuspected) patterns of possibilities which we have to strive to fulfil. This is a positive and meaningful philosophy which we shall discuss later. It is implicit in many ancient legends, notably in the medieval morality play wherein Death says to Everyman, 'Remember that your life is not your own; it is only lent to you'.

*   *   *

It was when I was riding complacently on the tide of material success that Chance played her most significant card. My activities were not entirely worldly, for I had sought inspiration in the tenets of Freemasonry and had become adept in its rituals. One evening, on returning from a Lodge meeting in a slightly exalted frame of mind, I met a neighbour out for a stroll. We engaged in a casual conversation which, quite unexpectedly, developed into a discussion of some refreshingly new ideas. As a result of this encounter I was introduced to Dr Maurice Nicoll, whose philosophy opened up for me entirely new horizons.

Maurice Nicoll was a remarkable man who had studied psychology with Jung in Vienna and had become an acknowledged authority in the field. In 1921 he met the Russian philosopher P. D. Ouspensky, who was teaching a system of ideas promulgated by an extraordinary mystic, G. I. Gurdjieff. Dr Nicoll immediately recognised the truth of these ideas, and a year later abandoned his Harley Street practice to study at 'The Institute for the Harmonious Development of Man' which Gurdjieff had founded at Fontainebleau, later returning to England to operate his own school.

At that time, the ideas were only transmitted by personal instruction, though they have since received wide publicity. They are basically concerned with the development of real consciousness, to which we have a right, but which we do not normally exercise. I shall, of necessity, refer to some of these ideas as we proceed, though only in sufficient detail to provide a background to the concept of the real adventure.

In retrospect, I think the major impact of his teaching was the realisation of the lamentable irresponsibility of my complacent philosophy. If life is indeed some kind of apprenticeship, one should at least try to discover to Whom one is articled! Under Dr Nicoll's guidance I gradually learned (and not without many rough attacks on my conceit) how to stretch my mind beyond the limits of its customary uncritical acceptance, and discover entirely more meaningful interpretations of the events of life.

*   *   *

This more alert thinking is spoken of in Christian theology as repentance, which means literally re-thinking; but the meaning has become degraded to imply regret for one's misdeeds, which is a useless activity. The word in the Greek is *metanoia*, implying expansion of the mind, which is altogether more significant. We have, in fact, to re-consider many aspects of life which are normally unquestioned.

For example, we take for granted that the phenomenal world —the world of appearances and events—is completely real, whereas it is actually no more than the shadow of a much more comprehensive reality. Our awareness of the world in which we live is derived entirely from the evidence of our physical senses, which are known scientifically to be very limited in their range of response. Indian philosophy says that we live in a world of *illusion* (maya). This does not mean that it is imaginary, for it evidently has a very real existence for us. The word illusion is derived from the Latin *ludere*, meaning to play a game; so that to say that the familiar world is an illusion simply means that it is a portrayal, in accordance with certain specific rules, of a much greater structure which is not manifest to the senses.

The existence of this unmanifest realm is implicit in the conventional idea of Heaven. We accept, as an article of faith, that the ordinary pattern of events, however interesting and even exciting, is in some way only a partial experience. Yet this can be much more positively interpreted by envisaging a superior realm which *embraces* the phenomenal world, so that the events of life are created by the interplay of conditions in this real but unmanifest world. This leads to the idea that one is *inhabiting* the life (and, ipso facto, the physical body).

There are many esoteric legends which convey the idea explicitly. One of the most beautiful is the Hymn of the Soul, which is found in the Apocryphal New Testament.* This describes the adventures of a prince who is sent into a distant and hostile country to recover a pearl which had been lost; but he is distracted by the conditions, and messengers have to be sent to remind him of his aim. This allegory contains the clear indication that earthly existence is not an end in itself, but a descent into an inferior region, to which one does not belong, and from which there is the possibility of return.

There appears to be an innate acceptance of this idea of return to the source, prompted perhaps by a vestigial memory of our real origin, but we do not understand how it is to be achieved. Our ordinary thinking is so firmly conditioned by the sense of time that we inevitably envisage the return journey in similar terms, involving the pursuit of a mystical goal to be attained in some undefined future state, *for which we are content to wait*. This is not really very intelligent. It is like planning a voyage to a far country and expecting to arrive without ever leaving harbour.

We need a more purposeful interpretation which regards the return as a progress not in time but in state or level. This is not an automatic process but demands a particular kind of effort

---

* This legend, also known as The Hymn of the Robe of Glory, is found in the Acts of Thomas, Apocryphal New Testament, translated by M. R. James, p. 411 (Oxford).

which we have to discover and then practise for ourselves. It is
as if there were some kind of ore, to be found only in this inferior
region to which we have descended, which if brought to the
surface can be refined by a superior intelligence. But like the
prince in the legend, we succumb to the hypnotism of the
environment and forget the real purpose of the exercise.

It was this idea of refinement which was the inspiration of the
mediaeval alchemists. They are customarily regarded as ignorant
charlatans seeking with indifferent chemical knowledge to trans-
mute base metal into gold. Actually their activities were merely
an external representation of a more subtle spiritual alchemy,
through which they endeavoured to make contact with higher
levels of existence. By pursuing the maxim of Hermes Trismegistus
—'Separate the fine from the coarse'—they sought to discover
the allegorical Philosopher's Stone which would be the key to
real understanding.

This simple aim has become submerged in the flood of
materialism. Yet the need for this spiritual alchemy is even more
urgent at the present time. We live in a disintegrating society in
which the increasing preoccupation with detail is leading us ever
farther from the truth. We have to check this headlong flight and
endeavour to make contact with the integrating influences in the
Universe.

Despite the technical and sociological developments of the era,
we cannot really alter the pattern of events, which is controlled
by cosmic influences. Our individual experience, though, can be
transformed in quality by the influence of higher levels of intelligence, so that one's life becomes the 'base metal' for an entirely
practical real alchemy.

* * *

This is the real adventure, as I shall endeavour to illustrate
from my own experience; and the first requirement is evidently
an adequate supply of raw material, in the shape of a wide and
varied experience of life. There is an Indian saying that one must
be 20 years a youth, 20 years a soldier and 20 years head of a

household before seeking understanding. The adventure cannot be undertaken by people who are shiftless or incompetent. We have to learn to contend with life, and to savour its experiences to the full.

Only when this has been done can we respond properly to superior influences. At the appropriate time these provide 'accidental' contacts, either personal or through the written word, with people who have already embarked on a real course. If we choose to respond to these ideas they can create the beginning of a new understanding.

However, this is no more than the beginning of what is essentially an individual adventure. For a time one has to rely on external instruction, and try to surmount the enormous weight of habitual associations. But these ideas, however inspiring, can do no more than set our feet on the way. We have to pursue them for ourselves, for the adventure is a journey—not in time but in understanding—which necessarily involves exploration. If we are content to rest in the contemplation of some idea which has been presented to us, believing that we have thereby achieved our goal, we shall find that it fades, and has to be re-sought.

The early stages of my own adventure were guided by Dr Nicoll, with a patience and affection for which I am profoundly grateful. It was not until after his death, when I could no longer sit complacently at his feet, that I realised the necessity to build for myself on the foundations he had laid; and having taken up my own cross (as he had more than once enjoined me to do), I began to encounter an ever-widening range of ideas of a quality far beyond my early understanding.

This is a practical task, involving a continuing endeavour to respond to the authority of the higher levels within us, which are permanently in touch with reality.

* * *

Despite the prevailing opinion of the masses today, nothing in the Universe is free of charge. There is a Spanish proverb, which runs, 'Take what you want, says God, and pay for it'. So we can realise that if we seek an expansion of consciousness it must be paid for by effort; and paradoxically, the greater part of this lies in finding what the required effort actually is.

We have to discover and practise new ways of thinking—the 'metanoia' mentioned earlier—but for a long time our efforts are nullified by expectation of result, so that many are discouraged and abandon the quest. The real operation is not in time, but is one which occupies the whole life. As one gradually begins to realise this, there is a complete change in the quality of one's experience. The difficulties are no longer regarded as obstacles to be overcome in a grim pursuit of future enlightenment, but are themselves the necessary elements of the exercise.

Jerome K. Jerome, in a light-hearted essay entitled "On the time wasted in looking before one leaps", says that life is to be *lived*, not spent. If we are able to discover this secret, life becomes a significant adventure having a curiously impersonal quality of delight.

CHAPTER TWO

THE UNMANIFEST WORLD

We have considerable difficulty in understanding what is meant by 'thinking in new ways'. We are apt to believe that this involves discarding one's habitual associations in favour of supposedly more intelligent interpretations. This is a sterile approach, how-ever, because we are still standing on exactly the same ground; real ideas are of a different, and superior, quality. Hence we do not have to abandon ordinary knowledge. On the contrary, we should increase it, but at the same time learn how to integrate it within an entirely superior pattern of reality.

We have to start by examining more closely the basis of ordinary knowledge which we normally take completely for granted. How, for example, do we know that we are alive? Our awareness, such as it is, is derived primarily from impressions received by the senses. These are co-ordinated in the brain, which then dictates the appropriate response. It is a mechanism of remarkable complexity and elegance, which we will discuss in more detail in the next chapter; but the significant feature is that these senses only operate within an extremely restricted range.

Our eyes, for example, respond to a small band of (invisible) radiations called electro-magnetic waves. A vibration at a rate of 400 billion per second produces a sensation of red, while as the frequency increases, the sensation of colour runs through the familiar spectrum culminating in violet at 750 billion. But this is only a tiny fragment of the total of such waves known to science, which range from physiological phenomena such as brain rhythms through the gamut of radio waves, infra-red waves (which produce the sensation of heat), the regions of ultra-violet waves,

X-rays, gamma rays and the like, to the incredibly fine cosmic rays which reach us from outer space.

These waves permeate the physical world, but a certain very small selection, within the band called visible light, becomes entangled with the atomic structure of various substances and is thereby reflected in whole or in part, producing the appearances of shape and colour. But clearly if our eyes responded to a different range of vibrations—such as X-rays—the apparently solid objects of the familiar world (including its occupants) would disappear, and would be replaced by a completely different environment.

There is a similar limitation in our sense of hearing. The ears respond to a different kind of vibration, produced by a jostling of the molecules of the air within a normal range of about 30 to 16,000 vibrations per second (though as we grow older we become progressively less sensitive to the higher frequencies). Yet birds and animals have different ranges of hearing, a familiar example being the 'silent' dog whistles which produce sounds beyond the range of human hearing, but to which the dog immediately responds. Bats use a radar system employing supersonic vibrations of a still higher frequency, while there are many industrial processes which use molecular vibrations far beyond the limits of audibility.

All the senses, in fact, are severely limited in their response and this restriction is deliberate because the brain can only cope with a limited amount of information. Hence they only supply sufficient information to maintain an adequate relationship to the environment. Other organisms have similarly restricted, and different, ranges of sense appropriate to their situation in nature, and there is a certain correlation between brain size and sensory range. This can be regarded as resulting from the normal process of evolution, though in my view physical evolution is itself merely the implementation of a design directed by a superior intelligence.

The fact remains that our awareness of the world in which we live is derived from the interpretations of information supplied by a very limited range of senses. Hence these interpretations must be regarded as conveying only a fractional understanding of reality. Moreover, there is here an important but usually unrecognised corollary. We have invented many devices, such as microscopes and telescopes, which greatly extend the range of observation, but the information which they provide is still co-ordinated by the exercise of sense-based reasoning. So that, although today we possess a very detailed and indeed fascinating knowledge of the physical world, this is by its very nature fundamentally restricted.

This is not the conventional view, which regards material knowledge as absolute—though as we shall see later this belief is no longer rigidly held. It is important, nevertheless, to know something about the intricate patterns of modern scientific knowledge which, by their very elegance, provide clear evidence of a superior intelligence. This knowledge itself awakens the innate sense of wonder and mystery which Einstein, in "The World as I see it", calls the fairest thing we can experience, without which man is like a snuffed-out candle.

One of the tasks which Dr Nicoll gave me was to prepare for the group a series of lectures on scientific subjects. As I did so, I found that the conceit of my vaunted knowledge began to give way to a sense of delight in the beauty of the structures. I spoke of the basis of chemical compounds which is derived from a remarkable pattern of harmony; of the structure of the elements which obeys an octave pattern of continuous creation to which we shall refer later. I spoke of the mystery of the electron and the patterns of vibrations within the Universe, and other ideas which I subsequently published in a book entitled *The Universe of Relationships.*

One of the most significant concepts of modern science is that the familiar world is mostly empty space. The material objects of our environment are assemblies of sub-microscopic atoms separated by relatively enormous distances. These atoms are themselves miniature solar systems comprising even more minute entities called electrons, revolving in orbits round a central nucleus, again at relatively enormous distances. The separations, in fact, are comparable in their scale with those in the macroscopic world of the actual solar system. Moreover, neither the electrons nor the nucleus are considered to be material particles but are regarded as minute disturbances of the all-pervading but intangible fabric of the universe.

Hence it is clear that the physical world is indeed an illusion of the senses. Not only its appearance but its behaviour is a translation, in terms of sense-based intelligence, of the conditions existing in a superior, but unmanifest, realm, which the philosopher Immanuel Kant called the *noumenal* world—the world of the mind. Moreover, as we shall see, the conditions in this real world are subject to laws of a different order, directed by a correspondingly higher consciousness.

It is here that real knowledge exists and is understood, by beings of a higher level who inhabit the region in the same way that we inhabit the phenomenal world. Various names are given to these beings in different theologies. Gurdjieff called them the Conscious Circle of Humanity, responsible for the esoteric teachings promulgated through the ages, sometimes by specific messengers, sometimes through the inspiration of individuals who have achieved contact with this higher level.

* * *

The sense-based mind will tend to regard these ideas as speculation, not to be accepted without proof. This is superficially reasonable, for the whole development of human knowledge is based on intelligent conjecture which one then endeavours to verify by experiment. But the noumenal world is, by definition, a realm directed by laws of a superior order which cannot be understood in conventional terms.

This does not automatically disprove its existence. On the contrary, it confirms that the real world is not just an extension of the conventional pattern. New concepts are therefore required and it is now acknowledged that we are equipped with response mechanisms additional to the physical senses, which can communicate directly with the noumenal world. We shall have occasion to refer to these paranormal faculties as we proceed (and specifically in Chapter 7, which deals with what is called extra-sensory perception). It will suffice to note here that these senses—which are not abnormal but exist *side-by-side* with the conventional senses—are concerned with what we call intuition, all too often ignored in the avid pursuit of 'facts'.

The most encouraging aspect of scientific thought today is its growing recognition that life cannot be explained in terms of itself. Nature has a curious trick of refusing to provide logical answers to questions which go beyond certain limits. Any system, in fact, only retains its characteristics within the limits of its scale. This notion was expressed clearly by the Swiss physicist Eugene Guye, who said 'The scale of the observation determines the phenomenon'. As a result, science is continually coming up against imponderable barriers which can only be surmounted by the formation of new concepts and is thereby being gradually forced to admit the existence of superior levels of intelligence. As Arthur Koestler has said, the greatest physicists of our century have been acutely aware of the occult nature of the concepts with which they have operated, and have sought a synthesis between the exact science of physics and man's intuitive intimations of deeper levels of reality.*

*　　*　　*

This is the point at which one encounters the innate sense of mystery. The first great mystery about man is that he is not his body, which is merely a temporary residence. As an entity in the phenomenal world it is subject to many complex laws, of which today we have a considerable, though by no mean complete, knowledge. But his real part lies within the unmanifest realm, subject to laws of a different (and incommensurable) order.

There are various names for this immaterial part of a man, which is actually a composite structure containing several levels. Gurdjieff called it, quite simply, *Essence*, which he defined as the real part of a man, with which he is born, and which there-

* The Roots of Coincidence (Hutchinson).

fore belongs to him, as distinct from his *Personality*, which is acquired and consequently has a purely transient reality.

According to this formulation, Essence originates from a very high level of the Universe (which is, for us, Divine), but is undeveloped. It thus has to receive some kind of nourishment, and we shall see that this can only be provided by the transmutation of the experiences of life in the phenomenal world. Hence the first requirement, as was said earlier, is to acquire substantial practical experience, resulting in the formation of Personality. This is the necessary 'first education', which should be wide and comprehensive to ensure an adequate supply of raw material for transformation.

However, there is a certain excitement in this activity which has a hypnotising effect. We come to derive our meaning increasingly from these acquired experiences and forget that they are merely a (necessary) kind of clothing. Moreover, we begin to bedeck ourselves in a host of unnecessary garments, attributing to ourselves a wholly imaginary sense of importance which is very easily assailed. This creates what is called False Personality, which has no reality whatever, but which we defend assiduously, to the point of becoming deeply offended by any attack on its validity.

All this clothing has to be stripped off at death, and if we have completely identified ourselves with this spurious reality the process will be very painful. It is therefore important to discover how to shed the many unnecessary garments while one is still alive.

* * *

We are led to the surprising realisation that the basic purpose of *individual* man is simply the development of his Essence. This seems very insignificant by comparison with the grandiose ideas of his destiny as master of this planet. Yet in fact it is all that he can do. It is only growth of Essence which can provide a meaningful contribution to the requirements of the noumenal world.

Social and scientific progress is the function of humanity as a whole, serving a cosmic purpose. Within this, individual man has to play his appointed role by the development of an adequate and competent Personality. But this expertise, fascinating though it may be, is no more than the raw material for his real development, which is an activity on a different scale not concerned with personal advancement.

In a condition of complete identification with life, which in esoteric language is called a state of sleep, Essence cannot receive the nourishment it requires and so does not grow. It needs a certain transformation of the available energies, analogous to the cooking or preparation of the physical foods which the body eats. This is the alchemy, to achieve which a 'second education' is required, creating a different understanding of the necessary events of life. It begins with the realisation that these possible transformations are *not* accomplished automatically. As will be seen later, man is created a self-developing organism, so that, according to the rules of the game, he is required to discover and exercise the techniques for himself.

Clearly this cannot be done without help. Fortunately there are influences continually available from higher levels, from which assistance can be derived once a man has awakened from his sleep. This is represented in many aspects of esoteric symbolism, as for example in Fig. 1 which is taken from the Mutus Liber* and shows angels with trumpets endeavouring to awaken the sleeping man. The Hymn of the Soul mentioned earlier contains the same idea. The prince, having forgotten his aim, is reminded by a messenger from his Father's court in the shape of an eagle, which he says, in a delightful phrase, 'alighted by me and became all speech'.

Here is the beginning of the real endeavour, by which the experiences of life are integrated into a much greater and more significant pattern.

* The Mutus Liber is a 17th-century book, of 'images without words' containing clues to the discovery of the Philosopher's Stone.

Fig. 1
Symbolic Representation of Sleeping Man (from the Mutus Liber*)*

CHAPTER THREE

THE HUMAN COMPUTER

As intimated in the previous chapter, my early efforts to change my thinking were based on the assumption that my previous ideas had to be discarded in favour of more lofty concepts. I began to be half-hearted in my business and domestic activities, believing that they were merely illusory and therefore unimportant. This only had the effect of making my behaviour exasperatingly unpredictable, with satisfaction to nobody, least of all myself. Gradually I realised that my conventional attitudes were not only competent at their level, but were necessary to a proper performance of my duties, and I had to work hard to recover the lost ground.

It is not the way of life which has to be changed, but one's interpretations of the situations. To achieve this, we have first to observe the existing reactions, without trying to alter them, for until they are properly recognised, any attempt to modify them is neither intelligent nor profitable. But at the same time we can begin to develop new associations which have a different quality of meaning, and which will, in time, create different reactions. It is in the formation of these new associations that we have to stretch our minds, and it will become evident that they are not concerned with conventional attitudes but with the entirely superior relationships of the real world.

Moreover, this new associative pattern can be formed, and responded to, *simultaneously* with the performance of one's ordinary duties, which thereby become integrated within a more coherent framework; but to understand this we must consider, quite simply, the basis of human behaviour which we normally take for granted.

*　　*　　*

One may make a start by examining the remarkable mechanisms by which we are related to the world in which we live. As said earlier, these are primarily derived from the translation of impressions received by the senses. They are mechanisms of a truly elegant design which respond to stimuli of various kinds generated in the phenomenal world. The eye, for example, responds to the stimulus of light. It is far more, though, than a mere detector, being provided with a lens of transparent tissue by which the image of a scene is focused onto a sensitive screen, called the retina, containing some 130 million separate photocells which detect the relative intensity (and colour) of the myriad elements of which the scene is composed. Electrical impulses are transmitted from each of these individual sensors to the brain, where they are co-ordinated into a recognisable pattern.

To do this, however, the brain has to be instructed. How does it know that a random agglomeration of signals from the retina represents, say, a tree, a house, a person—and more specifically, a particular tree, house or person? The incoming impressions are individually insignificant. It is only when they are co-ordinated within some established framework that the overall response has meaning.

It is necessary to make a similar translation of the impressions received by the other senses. A certain assembly of noises becomes recognised as, say, a voice or a bird song, while sensations of touch, taste and smell are only meaningful in comparative terms. The whole gamut of impressions received by the senses every second is translated by the brain (or more correctly, by the central nervous system which includes the solar plexus and the spinal cord) with reference to an established network of *associations*, in accordance with which it dictates appropriate courses of action.

This associative network is extraordinarily complex, and

(except for certain instinctive functions which are discussed later) has to be *acquired by experience*. Thereafter it is taken for granted. Indeed, the extent of these automatic (and unconscious) translations is normally completely unrecognised, a particularly interesting example being the inversion of the visual image.

When we see an object, the lens of the eye produces an image on the retina which is upside down (as in a camera) and the brain has to be educated to invert this information. The process can be observed in a small baby beginning to relate itself to its surroundings. It tries to touch its feet by raising its arms above its head, but finds that this does not produce the right result. By experience the brain learns that the information has to be inverted, which it thereafter does automatically. Interesting experiments were made some years ago by Dr J. Stoyva, of the University of Colorado, to confirm that this was in fact an acquired translation. A man was provided with glasses which deliberately inverted his vision. At first this entirely confused his reactions but after a short while his brain became re-educated and he was able to undertake his customary activities quite normally. When the inverting lenses were removed he again suffered a temporary derangement of his faculties, but the recovery time was shortened because the brain remembered its former long-established translations.

This quite remarkable mental re-orientation is but one example of a whole range of interpretations by which the brain relates us to the world in which we live. It is a virtually instantaneous and entirely automatic process, not requiring any conscious attention, and indeed to try to think about the operations in detail would simply bring the system to a shuddering halt. But it is possible to be aware, in a more detached and emotional part of the mind, of what is going on. For example, at this moment I experience a sense of wonder at the stupendous co-ordination which is directing my hand to express in writing the ideas I am trying to convey. Further, this kind of awareness can exist without detracting from the actual performance.

Moreover, the process is not confined to the recognition of objects. We acquire an elaborate pattern of psychological associations concerned with our relationships to people and events, and these entirely modify the translations produced by the brain. For example, I may see a shape which I recognise as Mr A, but this is immediately adulterated by judgments, of like or dislike, of whether he can be useful to me and similar considerations. There is a spontaneous reference to an acquired pattern derived from experience and memory, and it is this which determines my reactions to him.

This is again an automatic and *unconscious* process which provides the pattern of our relationships to other people. But there is here an additional degree of freedom, for one does not have to accept the translation. It is possible to exercise a certain directed awareness which can challenge the unconscious reactions. One can begin to recognise that the interpretations are not true, but are coloured by personal motives, so that I do not see Mr A as he really is, but as a creation of my own imagination.

This applies not only to personal relationships but to events in general, our interpretations of which are very largely derived from incorrect translations by the brain of the impressions received by the senses. This does not mean that the brain is defective or inadequate, but simply that it is wrongly directed. It is important, therefore, to examine its mechanisms more closely.

*   *   *

The manner in which the brain produces its elaborate sequence of responses to the received impressions has been the subject of considerable study in recent years and it is evident that the brain is in fact a highly sophisticated computer. Now, although computers are popularly regarded as examples of technological wizardry, they are basically assemblies of simple two-state devices which answer yes or no to questions put to them. They act like gates and are usually provided with several inputs, so arranged that if all the inputs are in a 'yes' condition the gate is opened and a 'yes' output is obtained. By using a suitable number of these gates, appropriately interconnected, answers can be obtained to a wide variety of questions, provided that these can be formulated in terms of yes or no.

With an adequate number of these gates, suitably arranged, complex analytical functions can be performed in incredibly short times, the individual operations usually occupying less than one millionth of a second. Moreover, all or any part of the information can be stored until required, and in this way the functions of memory are achieved. Since the brain contains millions of these gates, called neurones, its possibilities are clearly enormous.

The performance of any computer, however, depends essentially on the correct presentation of the information to be analysed, with regard not only to the original inputs, but even more to the direction of the subsequent operations. The computer, in fact, has to be provided with a *programme*, and until this is done it cannot function. Once such a programme has been established, the computer will continue to operate without further attention, answering any questions submitted as long as these are within the ambit of its programme. It can even be instructed to adapt its performance to cope with minor changes in conditions, but it *cannot create its own programmes ab initio*, since this requires the exercise of an independent and superior level of intelligence.

The reactions of the brain are determined by similar programmes, which ought to be directed by a superior level of intelligence, which we call the *mind*. In practice, this control is only exercised to a limited extent. This point is discussed more fully in Chapter 5. There is a reasonably adequate direction of the instinctive functions which maintain the life of the organism, but the voluntary behaviour is not subject to any conscious control. We respond almost completely to programmes which, once established by experience, become stereotyped, so that we are ruled by habit and not by intelligence.

The paralysing effect of habit was demonstrated in some remarkable experiments described by V. B. Droscher in his book *Mysterious Senses* (Hodder & Stoughton). As is well known, bats, which are nocturnal creatures, do not rely on sight during their flight but are guided by a radar system based on the emission of pulses of supersonic sound waves which are reflected from obstacles in the path, and permit appropriate avoiding action to be taken.

A bat was encouraged to take up residence in an artificial cave and means of observing its actual flight within the cave were installed. A convenient perch was included on which the bat quickly learned to roost. A series of obstacles was then introduced on the way to the roost which the bat avoided without difficulty. After a short time it developed a consistent flight path which it followed every time it came home to roost.

The obstacles were then removed one by one. This produced a surprising result in that the bat did not change its homing flight but continued to avoid obstacles which were no longer there. Finally, the roosting perch was removed. The bat homed by the same stereotyped course, and fell to the ground!

This is a most illuminating example of the formation of habit programmes. Having established a satisfactory route to the objective, no need arose to alter this, even though it was no longer necessary. This is completely typical of the normal run of human behaviour, which is entirely controlled by unconscious habit. I recall the amusing if trivial case of a man who went to collect something from his bedroom, but found himself in the lavatory because this was where his body usually took him on his way to bed each night.

All our ordinary behaviour is governed by long established habits, of which we are normally quite unaware. We see them in other people, and often use them to our advantage. I am often amused by the tactics of people who want something from me and who play on my expected habitual reactions. But there are, of course, many occasions when I am not so aware.

We have seen that the basic programmes are designed to permit minor modifications derived from experience and memory. Some of these are necessary, but a very large proportion are not. In any case, the reactions are entirely automatic, so that though a man may believe that he acts consciously, his behaviour is actually completely circumscribed by this established pattern.

This is so large that in any situation trivial alternatives exist, so creating the illusion of freedom of choice. It is a fallacy, for as long as the programme remains unaltered, everything happens in the only way it can happen.

It is, of course, possible to change or modify the programmes, permitting a greater realisation of the enormous potentialities which exist, but this requires a more conscious direction, which cannot be provided until the existing situation is properly understood. We have to learn to recognise, *and live with*, our behaviour pattern, for this is what relates us to our environment. I once saw that if I could change my reactions completely I should lose all my friends, who like me for what I am. Not that this would necessarily be a bad thing, for with a greater awareness one begins to establish new and more significant relationships.

*   *   *

It is evident that our behaviour, both physical and psychological, is controlled by mechanisms of remarkable complexity and intelligence which should evoke a keen sense of wonder, but are usually taken for granted. Moreover, in the ordinary way, we identify ourselves completely with these activities, believing that we *are* this machine. Our feeling of ourselves resides entirely in the body, and even our spiritual emotions are deemed to arise within this shell.

There is an innate belief in some immaterial entity which in some way accompanies us, but in the maelstrom of life it appears to have little place and so we assume that it is concerned with some future state of existence. Such was certainly my experience in early life, during which time I paid lip-service to conventional religion, but had no feeling of the immediacy of this superior level.

The concept of a real but unmanifest structure which *inhabits* the physical body is a much more inspiring, and practical idea. One begins to understand the body and all its works as a mechanism of remarkable precision and intelligence, but some-

35

thing which is not the only, and certainly not the most important part of oneself. This creates new meanings involving a range of superior possibilities which can be utilised now. We shall see, in fact, that it is only now that these possibilities can be realised, for after death they do not exist in the same way.

CHAPTER FOUR

THE LIVING UNIVERSE

A particularly happy part of my experience is concerned with flying, which I took up as a hobby in the days when it was relatively new and adventurous. I learned to fly in 1934 with Geoffrey de Havilland, whose joyous enthusiasm was most infectious. I like to feel that when he met his death many years later, attempting to break through the sound barrier, flying was still for him a great adventure.

My own progress was on a more humble scale. I joined the Herts and Essex Aero Club, where I made many friends and collected various trophies in the competitions which they organised, including one memorable year as Club Champion. The war put an end to private flying, but in 1947 I bought my own aircraft and spread my wings again.

Flying a light aircraft is an exhilarating experience. Apart from the joy of achieving perfect co-ordination with the machine, it introduces a new dimension into one's experience. One sees all at once possibilities which, at ground level, are developing in sequence, or may not even exist. I remember once taking a friend on a flight over a route which he frequently travelled by car. He was amazed to see the many places and situations on either side of the route of which he had been quite unaware on his normal journeys. On another occasion, flying over the convolutions of the Loire, I observed the wake of a river steamer still affecting one of the reaches, although at ground level the cause was no longer in sight.

Such apparently trivial impressions produce a momentary expansion of consciousness which immeasurably enriches the

37

experience. They awakened in me a certain emotional appreciation of levels, though this remained mainly superficial until a
casual incident led indirectly to a deeper understanding.

I had been attending a somewhat convivial rally at Tours and
on the return lost my way. Since I was running low on petrol,
I decided to land in a field to find where we were. Unfortunately
the field was unexpectedly bumpy and one of the undercarriage
supports broke. To add to the confusion, I found myself embroiled
with the local gendarmerie, from whom I was rescued by a
member of a local flying club. Meanwhile my passenger, with the
assistance of the spectators who always appear from nowhere on
these occasions, had tied up the undercarriage with rope and we
were able to resume the journey.

I later received a cutting from the local newspaper which
referred to an aircraft which had appeared over Brionne and
"semblait désorienté". This amused Dr Nicoll, who said it
described me completely. When I asked why, since I did not
regard myself as particularly disoriented, he retorted, "You still
get things upside down. You put matter before mind."

At first I felt this to be a quite unjust criticism, until I realised
that although I accepted the idea of a Universe of levels, I
envisaged it as starting at the bottom, each stage being an extension of the one below, which is the exact opposite of the truth.
Yet this upside-down thinking is characteristic of all our ordinary
attitudes. We are concerned with events rather than causes, inter-
preting everything in self-centred terms. We have an illusory
feeling of individuality on an earth which, despite what the
astronomers say, is still the centre of *our* universe. We may accept
intellectually that the transit of the sun through the heavens is
an illusion produced by the rotation of the earth on its axis, but
for ordinary purposes this is an academic, and unnecessary
abstraction. The sun, for us, rises in the east and sets in the west.

Science provides us with a certain enlargement of scale. It says
that the earth is merely one of a number of planets revolving
round a particular star called the Sun. Yet this whole solar system
is but one of some 1,000 million similar systems which make up
the galaxy known as the Milky Way (from its appearance to our

eyes as a tenuous streak in the night sky). Even this is only one of 10,000 million such galaxies in the known universe. The extent of the vast concourse is prodigious, involving distances so great that the light from even the nearest stars, travelling at 186,000 miles per second, takes many years to reach us.

At the other end of the scale we are told that all matter is a micro-universe of 'atoms', which are not solid particles but miniature solar systems embodying electrons revolving round a central nucleus in relatively enormous orbits; so that this 'too-too solid flesh' is mainly empty space populated by infinitesmally small local disturbances, having dimensions which are measured in million-millionths of a millimeter.

Now, although these concepts have significance for the physicist or the astromoner, they do not convey any real meaning for the ordinary man or woman. Indeed, they often create a wrong feeling of insignificance. Yet they are no more than extensions of sense-based intelligence containing no real awareness of levels. To obtain a properly-oriented understanding we have to start *at the top* and envisage a structure progressing from simplicity through successive stages of multiplicity.

* * *

Conventional thinking regards the physical universe as an accidental phenomenon which is slowly exhausting its potentialities and will ultimately revert to chaos. Real knowledge says that this is an illusion of logical intelligence and affirms that the Universe is a *living* entity embodying a succession of levels devolving from a Supreme Intelligence. These successive levels form a kind of ladder down which energy is transmitted from the Source, and is returned (in modified form) by a subsequent ascent.

This is an idea which is implicit in the very word 'universe', which means, literally, turning to unity, and is found in many ancient teachings, notably in the legend of Jacob's ladder. This records how in a certain place (which is significant) Jacob dreamed of 'a ladder set up on the earth, and the top of it reached to heaven : and behold the angels of God ascending and descending on it. And behold, the Lord stood above it.' (Genesis 28, 12.) The rungs of the ladder represent different levels which, while separate and distinct, permit the transference of energies in both directions. This is actually a rhythmic process, spoken of in Hindu philosophy as 'the breath of Brahma', which invigorates the whole structure. The Universe is not some gigantic accident, but a living creation, which is, at all its levels, a manifestation of the Deity.

We spoke earlier of the unmanifest world as the cause of the happenings in the phenomenal world, and one can apprehend the concept of a succession of intelligences of decreasing order in which each level is responsible for the creation of more detailed behaviour of the level beneath. Such a structure was formulated by Gurdjieff in what he called the Ray of Creation, and since this contains many ideas to which reference will be made in our explorations we must include a brief resumé here.

According to this formulation, the Universe is an *ordered* structure of 'world orders' created by the operation of two fundamental principles—the Law of Three and the Law of Seven. The first of these states that for any manifestation or happening *three* forces are necessary, in appropriate relationship. The well-known dictum that 'to every action there is an equal and opposite reaction' is only a partial statement, for without some reconciling force nothing can happen. Three forces are required, forming a *triad*, made up of an active or initiating force, which brings into play an opposing or passive force, with a third or relating force which transforms what would otherwise be a stalemate into useful action.

The highest point in the structure is the Absolute, a condition of unrestricted but Uncreate Unity, utterly beyond human comprehension. It is subject only to its own will and is therefore called World 1, 'without form and void', in the language of Genesis. As a unity, it is in a condition of equilibrium in which the internal forces are in a state of balance. If it is to become manifest—i.e. to be displayed as a specific entity—this balance must be disturbed by the introduction of an appropriate third force. Hence the process of creation involves the union of *three* forces, as is depicted in the threefold aspect of the Diety found in many religions.

This produces the first order of creation, embodying all possible forms of manifestation. It is the highest level of *created* intelligence and consciousness, subservient only to the will of the Absolute; but it is not unfettered, since all its manifestations involve the three primal forces. It is designated World 3.

Each of the possibilities of this world order can be more specifically materialised by a further (but more restricted) operation of the Law of Three, resulting in the creation of a third world order under six orders of laws—three of its own creation, plus the three over-riding laws from World 3. It is therefore called World 6 and is clearly more complex, and at the same time more circumscribed, being subject to laws which are one degree more remote from the will of the Absolute.

From the material of World 6 a fourth world order is created, subject to 12 orders of laws—three from World 3, six from World 6 and three of its own; and by similar procedure further world orders develop under 24, 48 and 96 orders of laws. Here the development stops, since it constitutes a period controlled by the Law of Seven, which we can ignore for the moment. It introduces a curious pattern of harmony in the structure which is discussed in Chapter 11.

*   *   *

These successive world orders are levels of intelligence, each possessing its own consciousness, but if we are to grasp this concept in more than abstract terms it must be related to our own level of understanding. In these terms *part* of the activity of World 3 will be the overall direction of the whole physical universe, which is interpreted by our senses as an assembly of some 10,000 million galaxies. Its operations are not confined to physical relationships within the universe of man's astronomy, and it is evident that a full understanding of the interplay of influences at this level involves a consciousness of awe-inspiring majesty. We can only say that World 3 represents, for us, the virtually incomprehensible concept of all possible worlds.

The corresponding activity of World 6 is the direction of the individual galaxies, only one of which is relevant to our own situation, namely the galaxy known as the Milky Way. We can, in fact, regard the influences from the Absolute as radiating in a structure of individual rays, *one* of which embodies that part of the Universe which we inhabit.

Similarly, World 12 is an intelligence concerned, as a small part of its function, with the behaviour of the individual solar systems throughout the galaxies. It can be represented in our Ray by the physical Sun, but it is actually an intelligence of, for us, a prodigious order, since even in physical terms there are some ten million million million solar systems in the universe.

(Nevertheless, we shall see later that man contains within himself psychological material of this very high quality. This is the 'Divine Spark' which inspires the return to the Source, which is man's real destiny.)

Subservient to World 12 is the more detailed, but less intelligent level of World 24, which can be regarded as being concerned with the subsidiary planetary systems, followed by World 48 responsible for individual planets, with their satellites directed by World 96. It will be seen that each level involves manifestations of increasing multiplicity and thereby operates with a more restricted intelligence.

The structure, which is illustrated in Fig. 2, is clearly radically different from the conventional view, and logical thinking is inclined to regard it merely as a somewhat fanciful representation of scale. But if one will allow it to lie fallow in the mind, one gradually perceives that it is not incompatible with conventional ideas, but *includes* them within the much more inspiring concept of an *intelligent* Universe containing a series of evolving levels of consciousness.

Thus the level called World 48 is not simply the physical earth, which is only one of its manifestations. It is a level of intelligence which directs the appearance and behaviour of the whole phenomenal world. It is characterised by considerable com-

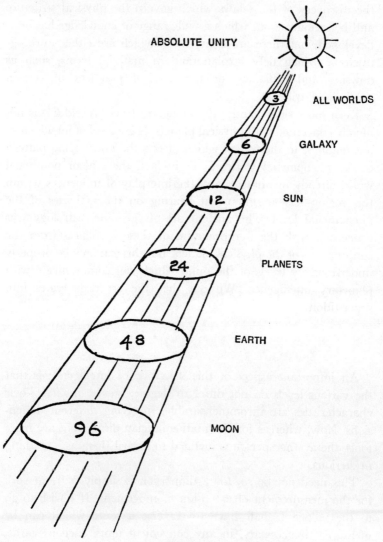

ABSOLUTE UNITY

ALL WORLDS

GALAXY

SUN

PLANETS

EARTH

MOON

Fig. 2
The Ray of Creation

43

plexity, and is under very many laws. Science is concerned with the discovery of those laws which govern the physical structure and behaviour, about which a wide range of knowledge has been developed, but there are many more which are either unrecognised or which defy 'explanation' in material terms, such as dowsing and radionics, or the magical practices of certain 'uncivilised' tribes.

Even more significantly, the planetary level (World 24) is not merely concerned with physical planets. It is a level of intelligence, not manifest to the senses, which directs the under-lying pattern of the phenomenal world. It is, in fact, the real or noumenal world already mentioned, and the interplay of influences within this region has an important bearing on the activities of the phenomenal level. The ancient art of (genuine) astrology was concerned with the interpretation of these influences from the conjunctions of the physical planets, but this can only be properly understood by levels of the mind which can communicate with planetary intelligence. Without this, the art degenerates into superstition.

*   *   *

An important aspect of this structure of intelligence is that the various levels do not differ in degree, but *in quality*. Their characteristics are incommensurable, involving different dimensions. Now, whereas for the mathematician dimensions are mere tools, the average person is inclined to regard them as something mysterious.

This need not be so, for a dimension is simply a framework for the measurement of extension or movement. If I wish to go to the village I shall have to traverse a route which can be measured, if necessary, in any convenient units, such as yards. Alternatively if I wish to specify the width of this page it can be expressed as so many inches. These are all units which relate to the dimension of length.

Suppose, however, that I wish to estimate how many lines of type the page will accommodate. This involves a measurement in a different direction, actually at right angles to the width. We may use the same units but they now have a different significance.

Two different orders of possibilities are involved, as illustrated in Fig. 3. AB is a line having a length of 10 (arbitrary) units. We can extend this line, say, 10 times in its own dimension, producing the line AB, which is 100 units long. It still remains a line (part of which we have shown dotted, since if drawn to scale it would run right off the page). However, if we move the whole line in a direction at right angles to its length, we create a *surface* ABCD, which is a phenomenon of a different order containing 10 units of length and 10 units of breadth. (If we want to assess its extent we can multiply the length by the breadth, which in this case would give us 100 units of area).

It will be clear that no extension of the line in its own dimension can ever create a surface, for which extension is required in a different direction, the dimension of breadth. On the other hand any two points in the surface can be joined to create a line in any arbitrary direction, such as XY; so that the surface contains the possibility of an infinite number of lines.

Two distinct and *incommensurable* orders of manifestation are involved. The additional dimension in the surface creates an entirely different degree of freedom which is not possible for the line. An intelligence operating within the surface can create, and understand, an infinite range of phenomena in the 'world' of lines, but any line cannot understand the surface in which it was created.

The same incommensurability applies through the hierarchy of levels in the Ray of Creation (and to any structure of levels). As the hierarchy is ascended, each successive level contains an additional degree of freedom. It is still subject to the same fundamental laws, but these are less circumscribed, so that it possesses a virtually infinite range of possibilities in relation to the level below.

*   *   *

The physical world contains three dimensions—length, breadth and height, by which we can completely specify the position and

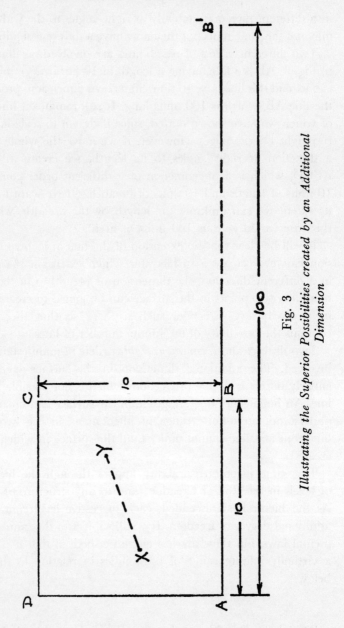

Fig. 3

Illustrating the Superior Possibilities created by an Additional Dimension

size of any object in space. The noumenal world, which embraces the physical world, contains possibilities beyond the evidence of the senses which can only be understood by the deeper levels of the mind. We can, however, achieve a partial understanding by *inference*—i.e. by reasoning from what we know. This is the way in which one can begin to stretch one's mind, imagining the sort of possibilities which might exist.

Actually, we unconsciously employ a degree of inference in daily life, for although we know by experience that we live in a three-dimensional world, our senses do not record the dimension of depth or distance *as such*. Our eyes register a series of flat shapes like a photographic print. By experience, assisted by our binocular vision, we learn to interpret subtle variations of shade and size as indications of depth. We accept these unconscious translations as matters of unassailable fact. Yet there are certain primitive tribes which have not developed this concept of depth. They see a bird close at hand larger than an elephant in the distance. This occasions no surprise, for they live in a world in which *some* birds are larger than *some* elephants—a world in which objects in general change their size and shape quite arbitrarily, and one in which they live quite happily.

By education and experience we have accustomed ourselves to a world containing a dimension which our senses do not actually perceive. By an extension of the process we can begin to form similar concepts of the real world containing still higher dimensions. This involves a further exercise of thinking beyond the senses, and because we are unaccustomed to it, a considerable effort is required.

There are recorded cases of people born blind but to whom sight was restored in later life. The effort of coordinating the bewildering visual impressions was so great that they had constantly to be encouraged to accept this new world which we take for granted. I once tried, as an experiment, to observe what I actually saw, without the automatic (and unconscious) translation which accompanies ordinary awareness. This involved a pattern of shapes and colours, varying in size and merging one into another. It was a completely meaningless pattern, and I found it impossible to sustain the effort for more than about a minute!

Normally, of course, meaning is provided by the coordination of the random shapes derived from education and experience. Having acquired this understanding, the translations are effortless. It is evident, however, that if we now attempt to interpret the familiar world in terms which involve still higher dimensions, we shall find this just as bewildering and difficult to accommodate as the blind people found in endeavouring to adjust to the concept of the three-dimensional world. We can, in fact, only achieve these superior interpretations by cultivating an understanding of the *reality* of higher levels. This will involve persistent and initially unsuccessful effort, and one is easily tempted to abandon the endeavour which, by ordinary standards, appears unnecessary.

However, this applies in any attempt to transcend one's habitual thinking, and immediate success cannot be expected; but with persistence, one begins to recognise this as part of the adventure. Christ warns his disciples of the difficulties they must expect to encounter, and reminds them of the need to persist, saying, "In your patience ye shall possess your souls".

* * *

It will be noted that man does not appear in the simplified diagram shown in Fig. 2. This is because he does not reside solely in any level but is a composite creation covering a range of levels. His body exists within the phenomenal level (World 48) but his spiritual part belongs to the higher levels of Worlds 24 and 12. This is why he possesses superior possibilities.

Actually, he exists within a 'side octave' which devolves from the level of World 12, and which constitutes his ladder of return to his origin. He is, in fact, a subordinate but potentially important element in the vast mechanism of transformation in the Universe, which is discussed in Chapter 12.

CHAPTER FIVE

CHANGE OF MIND

We find a certain delight in real ideas, a delight which arises from their germinal quality. They are like seeds which can burgeon into flower, if they are provided with suitable soil. This, of course, we believe we already possess, but actually our soil is of poor quality, and has to be tilled if the ideas are to flourish.

The situation is illustrated in the well-known parable of the Sower recorded by Matthew (13. 3). Some seed falls on stony ground and is 'eaten by the birds'. Some falls in 'places of little earth', where it flourishes rapidly, but is unable to withstand the heat of the sun, and withers. This represents the superficial acceptance of the ideas, with insufficient depth of purpose, so that they are always secondary to the supposedly more important requirements of life. Other seed is depicted as falling 'among thorns', which grow up and choke it. These are the many firmly-rooted attitudes of self-love which have to be eradicated if a truly fertile soil is to be prepared.

Now, this is a major task, because in the ordinary way we have our priorities wrong. We allow our attention to be absorbed in unnecessary pursuits which mask the real objective. One of the greatest stumbling blocks is the desire for result. A young woman with whom I wrote a number of short stories once said to me, 'I believe you are the sort of man who reads a book in order to come to the end'; which astonished me, for how else does one read? It was not until much later, after my arrogance had destroyed our relationship, that I understood what she had meant. For having pursued any experience to its end, what remains but desire for more? The savour of the experience, which is its real quality, is all too often thrown away.

We occupy ourselves with a continual quest for solutions and if these are not forthcoming we blame the circumstances, deluding ourselves with the belief that if these could be changed the difficulties would be resolved. The spurious activity is really a disease, which Zen Buddhism calls *tanha*—the 'thirst for becoming'. Any real progress involves a change of attitude, so that instead of attempting to alter the circumstances, one has to seek a change of *mind*.

This is the metanoia spoken of earlier, the literal meaning of the word being 'expansion of the mind'. It is more than mere thinking and indeed at once implies a change of level, for no objective assessment of a situation can be made in terms of the situation itself, any more than one can lift oneself up by one's shoelaces. To understand this though, we must question what we mean by 'mind'.

* * *

Our ideas of the mind are normally very vague. We assume that it is in some way part of the brain, but this is a superficial assumption, not supported by any evidence. We saw in Chapter 3 that the brain is a highly-sophisticated computer which translates the information supplied by the senses, and dictates appropriate responses. It is a remarkably intelligent mechanism, but it can only operate in accordance with established programmes which are initially provided by a superior order of intelligence, not contained in the mechanism itself.

Now we have also seen that the body is not the whole of a man and that his real and much greater part exists within a superior world, beyond the evidence of the material senses. One can therefore postulate that this directing intelligence which we call the mind is an attribute of this unmanifest realm, which the German philosopher, Immanuel Kant, called the *noumenal* world —the world of the mind, as distinct from the phenomenal, or displayed world; and it is this non-material mind which provides the programmes to which the body responds.

This is a concept of considerable significance, for since the unmanifest world is itself a structure of different levels it follows that the mind can function at more than one level, and can thus create programmes of an entirely different order from those which ordinarily apply. However, in our ordinary state of consciousness only the lowest level of the mind is operative, and even then only in a very perfunctory manner.

We said, if you remember, that the basic programmes in a computer can, in themselves, contain provision for minor modifications derived from experience. This is common practice in man-made computers, which are thus provided with a limited ability to think. Similar sub-programmes are developed in the brain and operate automatically, without any further direction by the mind, once the basic programmes have been established. For example, if I am driving through unfamiliar territory, there is a continual need to assess the various signposts in relation to the route chosen beforehand from my maps. This is quite competently performed by a sub-programme which has been previously acquired to deal with map-reading in general. I do not have to learn the technique afresh every time I make a new journey and the programme is sufficiently flexible to accommodate many variations in detail, including the negotiation of unexpected one-way systems or similar obstacles.

The day is made up of similar automatic activities. I had fish for lunch today, whereas yesterday I had meat. This does not mean that I have to re-learn the basic process of eating. The brain has been educated to deal with trivial variations without having to call upon the full intelligence of the mind, even at its lowest level. And so the mind *goes to sleep*.

Such is our normal state, in which the various activities are virtually mindless. We do not believe this (though it is clearly evident in the vapid posturings of modern pop groups), but all our ordinary behaviour is adequately, and even competently, directed by appropriate sub-programmes which require no more than perfunctory attention.

Indeed to involve the full mind in these mechanical operations is unnecessary and wasteful, like using a sledge hammer to crack

51

a nut. The mind should be used to create and direct more significant programmes, which it can do *simultaneously* with the performance of the normal duties of life.

*　　*　　*

It is popularly supposed that mind is the sole prerogative of man. This is an arrogant and insupportable assumption, since the noumenal world is not concerned only with humanity. Nevertheless, man is a special creation characterised by the possession of a complex mind which provides him with superior potentialities.

Medical research has established that specific regions in the brain are concerned with particular functions. These require separate programming which has to be provided by appropriate sub-divisions of the mind, which Gurdjieff called Centres. These should work in harmony, subject to an overall directing intelligence. We have seen, though, that this intelligence is asleep, so that the several minds work in an uncoordinated and even chaotic fashion.

This is an idea which attacks our complacency, for we normally believe that our behaviour is directed by a single and consistent mind. An understanding of the real situation reveals unsuspected and very practical possibilities, which we can begin to appreciate by considering very briefly the functions which are directed by these different minds.

Our ordinary activities are directed by four Centres, the first of which is the *Instinctive Centre*. This is concerned with the involuntary bodily functions such as breathing, circulation of the blood, digestion of food, growth and repair of tissue, etc. It directs the mechanisms of the senses and the resulting physical sensations, permitting those which are beneficial to the organism and rejecting those which are harmful. It has a complete understanding of the requirements of the body and should not be interfered with, though we often stupidly over-ride it, thinking we know better. The programmes provided by this Centre are *not* acquired by experience, but are innate in the organism and persist throughout the lifetime of the body.

There are then three further Centres concerned with voluntary activities. These are basically concerned with the functions of movement, feeling and thought, and the programmes which they provide have to be derived from experience. *Moving Centre*, for example, directs such activities as walking, writing, speaking, sporting activities, etc., which all have to be learned, but thereafter become completely automatic and are taken for granted.

Equally taken for granted are the processes of feeling and thinking which are non-physical (though they still involve physical patterns in the brain). These 'psychic' functions clearly require different kinds of programme which are supplied by two further Centres. The first of these is the *Emotional Centre*, of which the true function is the recognition of relationships, from which stem aesthetic emotions and the sense of wonder and beauty. It is a very important Centre, for it can communicate directly with the noumenal world. But it is grossly misused for, as we shall see, its functions are usurped by a wide range of spurious feelings based on self-love.

Intellectual Centre directs the processes of thought and reason. These are functions involving discrimination and logic, on which the whole fabric of factual knowledge depends; and since logical reasoning is necessarily deliberate, this Centre works much more slowly than the others. The simplest action is completed before one can even begin to think how it is performed, while our emotions are virtually instantaneous.

The intellectual mind, however, is not restricted to this ponderous mode. Its higher levels can work with energies of a more rapid quality which communicate with the emotional mind. This provides the instant overall assessment of a situation which we call insight, which transcends the laborious detail of logical thinking.

All the voluntary Centres, in fact, can work with different levels of consciousness. The lowest, or outer level relates us to the external world, while the highest or inner level can communicate with the real world. In between is a middle level which can, as it were, look both ways and so create programmes which can reconcile the external and internal worlds.

There is a fifth mind called *Sex Centre*. This is only minimally concerned with physical sex (which is normally quite wrongly exercised), its true function being the direction of certain psychic transformations which can only be understood when the ordinary Centres are working in harmony; until which time speculation is futile and even dangerous.

Finally there are two *Higher Centres* with which we are not normally in contact. They communicate directly with the noumenal world, but because of the incommensurability of this level their language is unintelligible to the ordinary minds until these are directed by a similar order of consciousness. It is here that our real task lies, for by awakening the higher levels of the ordinary mind we are gradually enabled to establish contact with this superior order of Intelligence and begin to apprehend for ourselves the real nature of existence. We then no longer have to rely on second-hand information for, as Christ said, 'the Kingdom of Heaven is within you'. *We have, though, to seek it.*

* * *

For a long time I interpreted these ideas purely academically, and while I appreciated the intelligence of the structure, I took it for granted as indicating the superiority of man over all other animals. It was not until much later that I realised that this complex mind was provided for a cosmic purpose (which I was very far from fulfilling). More significantly, it was only a small part of the Greater Mind which directs the whole Universe. The mind of man is only one of the many minds which control the behaviour of the hierarchy. Most of these are beyond human comprehension, but we can at least understand that all the activities of the physical world are actually directed by appropriate minds.

The phenomenal world is essentially a structure of response to stimulus, but these very responses are merely reactions to programmes which have initially been established by a superior intelligence. This is so even though the subsequent operation is entirely mechanical and permits the development of minor modifications. A typical example is the behaviour of certain long-stemmed flowers which turn their faces to follow the path of the sun. The stimulus here is the light which is sensed by the plant and translated into action in accordance with a pre-established programme. The leaves respond to a different programme which produces the remarkable process of photosynthesis by which plants convert light into matter.

If, in fact, we are prepared to be less egregiously self-centred, we find that Organic Life as a whole provides overwhelming evidence of a directing intelligence—called by the ancient Egyptians the Soul of Nature—which ought to arouse our sense of wonder. What has laid down the programmes which determine the behaviour of the various species, such as butterflies and moths, with their curious cycle of transformation from caterpillar to insect; or the activities of the honey bee, with its vital influence on pollination? What determines the distinctive shapes of different trees? What is the purpose of the vast structure ranging from viruses to elephants? I am reminded of a remark made to me by a friend who said, "Have you ever thought, if you were God, how many things you would not find a use for?"

We do not have to postulate individual minds for all these creations. There is, in fact, evidence to suggest that there are 'group minds' which control the behaviour of different species, of increasing sophistication throughout the range. One finds examples of this in the activities of insect colonies, such as ants and bees, which display an overall awareness transcending that of the individual members. There are many other examples of group behaviour, such as migration, or the periodic mass suicide of lemmings; and there is a curiously related intelligence among the snow owls of northern climates which feed largely on lemmings. In the ordinary way they lay four or five eggs a year, but in those years where there is *going to be* a mass suicide they only lay one.

These are but a few of the wide range of fully authenticated examples of group behaviour. To say that these activities are instinctive explains nothing but the mechanism. Nor does logical thinking provide any explanation for the bewildering variety of natural phenomena. A rose is different from a cabbage because it contains a different code in the nuclei of its cells, but this does not explain why. Yet the intelligence of Organic Life understands the necessity for both cabbages and roses in the complex structure. The materialist says that all this evolved by accident, but it is equally possible and more intelligent to suggest that this evolutionary process is directed by the mind of Organic Life as the most convenient way of utilising the conditions which exist. In an intelligent Universe, nothing happens by chance, but only appears to do so to the limited understanding of sense-based reasoning.

Nor is this evidence of intelligence confined to Organic Life. So-called inanimate matter is a similar structure of response to stimulus, in which the constituent elements interact in accordance with pre-determined programmes which are now well-known and form the basis of all modern technological achievement. These are taken for granted, though their very elegance must arouse a sense of wonder.

I have always been intrigued, for example, by the way in which the 100-odd chemical elements fall within an ordered arrangement called the Periodic Table. From the lightest element, hydrogen, which has only one orbiting electron in its atom, progressively more complex elements are formed by the addition of further electrons in a succession of octave structures. Any group of elements will only combine to form the many natural (and artificial) compounds in the world if between them their electrons form a completed octave.

Moreover, although our sensory perception only recognises the condition of these elements in the present moment of time, there is reason to believe that they are being continuously created from the tenuous raw material of 'empty' space. Is this all to be regarded as happening by accident? We need to be a little more inspired in our thinking and recognise that these patterns, and many others equally fascinating, are the result of programmes laid down by a superior intelligence in the noumenal world.

* * *

Change of Mind

These ideas must be interpreted with emotional thinking, for logical reasoning will quickly lose its way in a search for verification in terms of sense-based knowledge. The emotional mind recognises real truth without the need for elaborate detail, which can only distort the ideas. With this simpler understanding we can apprehend the concept of Greater Mind through which the successive orders of consciousness in the Universe direct the behaviour of the whole structure. Within these are subordinate minds concerned with the activities of particular manifestations.

Within this structure is man, endowed with the possibility of a special kind of evolution (which we will discuss later). For this purpose he is provided with a multiple mind designed to respond to more than one level of consciousness in the hierarchy. However, this response is not automatic but has to be awakened by individual effort. He can, therefore, be described as a *self-developing* organism.

Humanity in the mass is subject to the programmes which direct Organic Life as a whole, and in which man is individually insignificant. In his state of psychological sleep his behaviour is not directed by his own mind, but is controlled by the group mind of the species (as is all too obvious in the behaviour of mass assemblies such as football crowds). In this condition he is subject only to the laws and influences of the phenomenal world which are of a cosmic nature. His personal advantage here is of no account.

However, he is equipped with an individual mind of great potentiality, if he chooses to use it, and this can respond to influences within the noumenal world, wherein he has significance and purpose.

57

CHAPTER SIX

THE HOUSE IN DISORDER

We have seen that the body is merely a temporary habitation for a real entity existing in the noumenal world. However, a superficial acceptance of this idea is no more than a re-statement in more specific terms of the comfortable philosophy of conventional faith. To exercise a significant influence, the idea must become part of our day-to-day awareness.

This immediately poses the question "who is aware?" We customarily regard ourselves as a being made up of a physical body and a variety of personal characteristics, to which a distinguishing name has been assigned, which we usually refer to as 'I'. In my case it is called Reyner, or more intimately, Jimmy (though it was christened John). In the first war it was called Number 138601. Today it has been given a variety of other numbers by the different departments of bureaucracy. It is, in fact, a quite impersonal entity, but one with which I identify myself completely. This 'feeling of I' is actually quite fallacious, though it is normally unquestioned.

The physical body is usually taken entirely for granted, as a necessary adjunct to existence. We become a little aware of it if its functions are disturbed, but we ordinarily accept its behaviour without question. Yet it is a mechanism of remarkable precision which exhibits automatically a spectacular range of skills. It performs a variety of complex chemical feats in the processes of digestion and breathing. It operates the intricate electrical circuitry of the senses and the central nervous system and thereby directs all kinds of mechanical operations, most of them involuntary. Really it deserves more than a perfunctory recognition.

As an engineer I have often been impressed by the elegant simplicity of some of the mechanisms. Our sense of balance, for example, is derived from three tiny semicircular canals in the inner ear. These are filled with fluid and contain small tufts of hairs with tiny weights on the ends. These tell the brain which way up we are, and immediately register any change of attitude. I feel that if I had been entrusted with the design I should have devised some much more clumsy and elaborate solution!

There are many even more striking instances of an elegant design to which the distinguished biologist, Sir Charles Sherrington, referred with a profound sense of wonder in his Gifford lecture, 'The Wisdom of the Body'.* He finds clear indication of a controlling intelligence, for apart from the precision with which the body performs its functions, including the ability to repair accidental damage (sometimes to a quite major extent), it exhibits a remarkable prescience during the embryo stage. A single fertilised cell multiplies by successive mitoses into 1,000 billion cells, and, at given stages, these develop specific characteristics which cannot have been acquired by experience, because this has not yet happened. Some form bone, some tissue, some nerves, some become brain cells. Some form, in the darkness of the womb, eyes which *later* will see. Some form lungs which *later* will breathe. There is astonishing direction here by the mind of Instinctive Centre.

The physical body, in fact, is subject to a clear and consistent direction : but our psychological behaviour, involving the constant interplay of feelings and thoughts, and the resulting actions, is not so directed. We saw earlier that these activities are basically responses to an elaborate pattern of associations acquired by experience; but whereas these programmes should be subject to the overall direction of the appropriate mind, this control is absent because the mind is asleep. Hence there is no proper organisation of the mechanism, which reacts to an entirely arbitrary and often inconsistent selection of programmes, often derived from an inappropriate Centre.

Thus we think when we should feel, and vice versa. I may,

* Man on his Nature, by Sir Charles Sherrington (Penguin).

60

for example, see a flower in the garden and decide that it is not doing as well as last year and perhaps should be moved. I entirely miss the delicate impressions of its beauty and scent and certainly experience no sense of wonder. Or I may, in a state of anger or frustration, drive my car with Emotional Centre, over-riding the competence of Moving Centre—which is, to say the least, very unclever. From sheer expediency, Intellectual Centre may dictate a measure of control, but this is minimal and our state, in general, is that of a house in disorder.

Dr Nicoll used to say that we had a dumb blonde in the office who was continually putting incoming calls through to the wrong department. But in fact we do not have even this degree of awareness, because we identify ourselves completely with the behaviour of the machine. We say *I* think this, *I* feel that, *I* will do (or have done) something, ascribing all these activities to an imaginary self which bears our name and is believed to be in control.

So deeply-rooted is this feeling that it is practically impossible not to speak (and think) in terms of I. Yet this 'I' is many-sided. One necessarily reacts differently to the varying occasions of business and social life; and in either sphere one's relationship to other people easily changes. A feeling of good will can be turned into resentment by a chance remark or other accidental twist of events. It is evident that the 'feeling of I' is very arbitrary, so that one's behaviour is not directed by a consistent and single unity.

It is helpful to realise that every group of incoming impressions produces an appropriate response which will involve any or all of the thinking, feeling or moving functions. This, in effect, creates a small automaton which performs the required duty entirely competently within its terms of reference. This automaton will be brought into action every time the particular conditions are repeated. The activities may be useful though they are frequently irrelevant, but each and every one of these puppets is invested with the authority of oneself, and is thereby entitled to call itself 'I'.

Changing circumstances bring into play different I's which are not subject to any overall control, so that our behaviour is full of unconscious inconsistencies. We are, in fact, governed not by a single controller, but by a host of separate and often contradictory little I's.

*   *   *

This concept of I's makes a significant contribution to our understanding, though for a long time it remains a purely intellectual idea. The majority of our daily activities are so adequately performed by the appropriate automata, which have been educated by experience in their particular field, that we unconsciously identify ourselves with the operations; and since, by and large, the system works, we see no reason to question the assumption that there is a single I in control. We are, in fact, so hypnotised by events that we do not notice the many inconsistencies and changes of meaning which make up the pattern of our lives.

Yet occasionally one may experience a dramatic moment of truth. I recall an incident in my youth when I was taking home a woman with whom I had spent a pleasant, but expensive, evening. On the way, the car broke down in a most awkward spot and she began to grow increasingly anxious, finally suggesting that I should try to hire a cab. To this a voice said "I can't. You've cleaned me out". I was utterly shattered to realise that an 'I' in me could make such an ungallant remark without my permission.

Much later, I realised that what had been so shattered was itself an I, or group of I's, constituting an entirely imaginary picture of myself as a person who always did the right thing. We live in such illusions and only gradually perceive that our behaviour is entirely controlled by this multiplicity of little personalities which we believe to be ourselves.

These I's are not necessarily to be deplored. Indeed, many of them are both competent and useful. I have previously referred to my early attempts to establish myself in life, and as the years passed these activities were increasingly successful. I wrote many books on such diverse subjects as radio-communication and cinephotography. With the advent of television I began to experiment with this new development, which was expensive. So we augmented our limited resources by arranging demonstrations in stores and fun fairs, including the provision (at three weeks' notice!) of a display for the Johannesburg Exhibition in 1936.

In 1930 I was appointed by the Institution of Electrical Engineers to edit a new publication called the Students' Quarterly Journal—an assignment which lasted for 26 years and brought me into contact with many men of eminence in the profession. Concurrently, the development in technology prompted me to purchase a factory and embark on the manufacture of electronic equipment, which provided many exciting opportunities, including the development of an early form of electronic autopilot in collaboration with Smith's Aircraft Instruments.

All this activity involved learning many new techniques, including commercial practice, of which I had previously been ignorant. It required the (unconscious) formation of a large number of additional puppets, which, by education and experience, learned to handle the varying situations with reasonable competence. Each in its turn was invested with my authority, creating the illusion (accompanied by no small conceit) that the events were being directed by a single person called Reyner, or I; and if there were occasional inconsistencies, surely one is allowed to change one's mind?

This illusion of unity, from which we all suffer, might be tolerable if the various actors who occupy the stage in their appointed roles were subject to a proper control. But in practice it is evident that this is conspicuously lacking, mainly because the principal characters, who have an admitted expertise, are continually interrupted by 'extras' who have no business in the play. These are the many I's of False Personality which induce a whole host of irrelevant feelings and thoughts, creating a range of what Gurdjieff called wrong psychic functions.

These all stem, basically, from self-love, which translates everything in terms of personal benefit. We indulge in constant internal considering concerned with what people will think of us; we count the cost all the time, and make 'accounts' against people (or even the Universe) if we do not feel that we have been rightly treated; we justify our thoughts and actions, believing that we are always right. There is constant anxiety for the morrow, which entirely outstrips right and intelligent anticipation. There is idle imagination, usually preceded by the futile words 'if only', and so on.

These we can do without. They only dissipate our energy, so that these useless I's must be deprived of their spurious authority. An I, once created, remains in existence throughout the life, and will always be ready to take the stage if permitted to do so. The undesirable I's, however, can be starved, so that they no longer feed on our blood, as Dr Nicoll used to say. We no longer believe absolutely in what they say and do; which cuts them down to size. This permits the useful I's to function properly, and can even make room for the development of a real feeling of I which could exercise some control.

*　　*　　*

These I's of False Personality are brought into being by a host of spurious programmes laid down principally in Emotional Centre, which begins to acquire an entirely false set of values. The Intellectual and Instinctive Centres are each concerned with discrimination, and may thus be regarded as having a positive and a negative part, but this is not so with Emotional Centre which, in its pure form, is concerned only with relationships. However, from a very early age we begin to populate it with *self-emotions*, which are not only unnecessary but become harmful.

These are developed from the sensations provided by Instinctive Centre, which quite properly classifies them as pleasant or unpleasant according to whether they are beneficial or harmful to life; but as soon as one identifies with these purely objective sensations they generate a whole range of spurious patterns in Emotional Centre which create personal emotions such as joy, sympathy, affection, etc., together with corresponding negative emotions such as boredom, irritation, envy, jealousy, suspicion, anxiety, fear, and so forth. Moreover, there is no stability in the system; at any time one emotion can be replaced by its opposite. One may feel deeply in love with someone; but this can easily be tainted by suspicion and turn into hatred, either temporarily or permanently.

The dangerous quality of negative emotions is that they are self-sustaining. The simple incoming impressions are not translated objectively, but trigger a network of artificial associations based on self-love. This creates an entirely imaginary sequence of *internal* impressions which continues long after the original external impression has passed, and which blocks the entry of further true impressions and can even paralyse the system. In a state of acute anxiety, for example, one is unable to think, or act, clearly.

Our meaning is derived almost entirely from these spurious activities, which provide our criteria of enjoyment. This applies to many pursuits which we regard as innocuous, but even more to the vast array of negative emotions, which we regard as a quite normal and even palatable diet. In this way the daily intake of psychic energy is squandered on a variety of useless activities.

These stupidities are responses to programmes laid down in an *artificial* negative part of Emotional Centre which has no right to exist, and is a gross misuse of the available potentialities. In its pure state the Emotional Centre is clairvoyant, being aware of the real relationships in the noumenal world. These cannot turn into their opposite, like the personal emotions which is all we ordinarily experience, but embrace all the possibilities simultaneously. Such positive emotions are occasionally experienced in brief, unexpected moments, though with a properly nourished Emotional Centre they can be of a longer, and contrivable duration.

We shall refer later to the necessity for nourishing the mind. It is an unfamiliar idea which is not usually appreciated. I found no difficulty in observing the more obvious manifestations of I's in my behaviour, and even learned to suppress some of the more stupid ones; and for a long time it seemed sufficient to cultivate a steadily increasing awareness of the situation. There must be no judgment in the exercise, because this implies the belief that it is *oneself* which is behaving like this, whereas one is actually witnessing a cavalcade of puppets.

Gradually, however, I began to perceive a more positive field of endeavour involving a conscious use of the available energy. This may be done in two ways. Firstly by saving some of the energy which is so foolishly squandered in negative emotions and self-love. This requires the sacrifice of at least part of the spurious self-esteem to which one clings so unnecessarily, and this can create new energies which nourish the mind, as is discussed in Chapter 12.

Yet there is a further source of nourishment which is not usually recognised. All the activities so far considered are basically derived from the responses of the physical senses. As was said earlier, though, we possess a range of paranormal senses which do not have a physical basis but provide impressions of a superior quality. These exercise the intuitive faculties which nourish the higher levels of the mind. These in turn will provide new interpretations of situations, often involving connections between events which to the ordinary senses are separated in time or space.

These faculties are available to a much greater extent than is generally recognised, being part of the normal, but latent, equipment of the organism, and we shall discuss them in detail in the next chapter. It may be noted, however, that the paranormal senses cannot function if all the available energy is squandered in the wrong, useless, psychic functions. To allow them to develop, one has to silence the incessant clamour of the habitual I's and make room for ideas of a superior quality. In the words of the Psalmist—be still, and know that I am God.

CHAPTER SEVEN

EXTRA-SENSORY PERCEPTION

It will be appropriate here to consider in more detail the nature of the paranormal senses to which several references have been made in earlier chapters. The existence of a 'sixth sense' has long been recognised as responsible for what is often called second sight, but this is usually regarded as an abnormal faculty only possessed by people who are psychic or 'fey'. This is not so, for we are all equipped with a range of paranormal senses —i.e. senses which exist side-by-side with the physical senses— which we have a right to use, but which are customarily ignored.

Over the past few decades there has been an intensive study of extra-sensory perception, or e.s.p., together with the associated phenomena of telepathy, clairvoyance, pre-cognition and psychokinesis (the ability to move physical objects by thought). There is, in fact, an accepted science of parapsychology concerned with psi phenomena, as they are called, which has established the undoubted existence of communication between people and objects beyond the expectations of the laws of chance (which, paradoxically, are statistically predictable).

The pioneer work by J. B. Rhine, of Duke University, California, is now well known. He designed a series of five cards bearing distinctive emblems which were selected in random order while a subject in a separate room guessed which card was being presented. The proportion of success was significantly greater than would be indicated by statistical probability and this led to a wide variety of more sophisticated investigations by both Rhine and others.

It is not proposed here to discuss these developments in detail, partly because there is already extensive literature on the subject, to which reference may be made if desired. A more important reason, however, is that much of the work appears to be directed to a search for explanations of extra-sensory phenomena in terms of conventional reasoning. Now we have seen that all ordinary knowledge is fundamentally sense-based and hence is inherently limited. It seems to be accepted that paranormal faculties are directed by the mind, but this is all too frequently regarded as some kind of extension of the senses, whereas we have seen that the mind is a structure having several different levels. Any real understanding involves the recognition that the paranormal senses are directed by a level of the mind superior to that which governs the responses of the ordinary senses.

We shall therefore discuss extra-sensory phenomena from this aspect, and endeavour to discover the relationship of the paranormal senses to the real but unmanifest realm in which the true causes lie.

*   *   *

Let us first examine the nature and functions of the paranormal senses. As we have seen, the physical senses respond to impressions of various kinds received from the external environment, as a result of which information is communicated to the brain. This information deals with facts—i.e. the condition of things as they are at the moment of receiving the impression—and these facts are then correlated by the brain in accordance with its established pattern (which includes memory and reason), to provide an appropriate response.

The paranormal senses are concerned with information of a different character, dealing with *relationships*. They recognise patterns of cause and effect lying not merely in the immediate present but in the past and/or future—relationships which exist within the eternal fabric of the noumenal world. Thus the paranormal senses are not a mere extension of the physical senses but communicate with the real world and so provide information of a superior quality. However, the brain can only interpret this information under the direction of the higher levels of the mind. Since these are normally dormant, there is usually no adequate response.

Because of this it is very difficult to assess scientifically the extent and quality of these faculties; but it will be evident that they have much greater potentiality than can be measured by routine testing of phenomena which are regarded as abnormal, or at least peculiar. The truth is that we all possess these faculties, but have not learned how to use them. Even the fragmentary responses which do occur from time to time are usually ignored as unimportant or superstitious.

One tends to associate the paranormal senses with unusual manifestations such as clairvoyance and pre-cognition; but these are an exceptional exercise of the faculty, possible under suitable conditions as we shall see in Chapter 9, but requiring the direction of higher levels of consciousness with which we are not normally in touch. The paranormal senses can, and do, operate at more lowly levels, producing many effects in ordinary experience which we usually take for granted.

Why does one 'instinctively' like or dislike certain people? There are no facts available here. What is responsible for the 'atmosphere' of buildings or locations? A happy house is one which is permeated by pleasant associations, while one in which the inhabitants indulge in a constant expression of negative emotions acquires an evil atmosphere. One is instantly receptive of these extra-sensory impressions, which also respond to the psychological state of other people (though one is aided here by the physical impressions of facial expressions or posture).

There are other examples of this kind of sensitivity. Why, for example, do we sometimes know, without any apparent reason, that we are about to receive a letter from someone with whom we have had no contact for years? Why does one often know from whom a telephone call is being made before even lifting the receiver? These are trivial examples, which we normally attribute to coincidence; but actually they are the result of intuition (which women seem able to exercise more readily than men). More significantly, why do we sometimes know when to act, and when to wait? As the unknown author of *Ecclesiastes* wrote in the second century B.C. :

> To every thing there is a season, and a time to every
>   purpose under the heaven;
> a time to be born and a time to die;
> a time to plant and a time to reap;
> a time to kill and a time to heal;
> a time to break down and a time to build up;
> a time to weep and a time to laugh;
> ....
> a time to seek and a time to lose; a time to keep and
>   a time to cast away;
> a time to keep silence, and a time to speak.
>
> (Ecclesiastes 3, vv 1–8)

This is saying, quite simply, that the phenomenal world is a pattern of rhythms. Some are recognisable—as for example, the succession of the seasons—but others are more subtle, and not apparent to the ordinary senses which are tied to the immediate present. The paranormal senses respond to the pattern in the real world and so convey intelligence of a superior order.

From these brief examples it will be clear that there is nothing peculiar about extra-sensory perception. It is a natural function which has fallen into disuse because of our complete pre-occupation with facts. Yet it was employed as a matter of course by the wise men of old, and is still used today by certain so-called uncivilised tribes, notably the race of African pygmies described by Laurens van der Post in his book *The Lost World of the Kalahari* (Hogarth Press), who can communicate with each other over vast distances, and the Kahunas of Polynesia, whose priests practise a remarkable hidden magic called Huna, of which there is a fascinating account in Dr Aubrey Westlake's book *The Pattern of Health* (Watkins).

This secret science is based on a concept of different levels of intelligence and manifestation not unlike that which we have been considering, but we shall not discuss it in detail because we are concerned here with a more individual, if less spectacular, magic —to wit, the development of understanding. This is essentially a paranormal function—an exercise of the emotional mind—but it is usually confused with reasoning.

Reasoning is based on facts, marshalled by oneself. Understanding—standing under—implies the recognition of something higher than oneself and in its relation to other people can create the precious feeling of compassion. This is usually interpreted as having pity, but the word means literally to experience together (from the Latin *patior*), which has a much deeper significance.

The paranormal faculties can be stimulated by the use of drugs, but this is not a permissible exercise because, unless the brain has been adequately programmed by the deeper mind it will make nonsense of the information, and its normal functioning (particularly in respect of the physiological functions normally controlled by Instinctive Centre) will be jeopardised. Moreover, even if drugs, such as L.S.D., produce moments of enlightenment, the experience is transitory because one has not paid for it (in psychological coinage) and hence is not allowed to keep it.

We know well enough what payment is required, if we choose to make it. Paranormal sensitivity is not developed by 'taking thought', for the faculty already exists, but is atrophied from lack of use. We have to begin to nourish the emotional mind by withdrawing some of the precious energy which we habitually squander in the activities of the self-love.

*   *   *

There is an aspect of extra-sensory perception which is of considerable practical interest, namely the art of divining or dowsing, which is of immemorial antiquity. This is the art of obtaining information not available to the ordinary senses by allowing the paranormal senses to influence some simple indicating device. Cicero describes the practice of taking auguries by casting bits of stick, while as early as the 15th century prospectors in the Harz mountains of Germany were using divining rods to locate hidden deposits of water or minerals.

The usual form of rod was a forked hazel twig which when held in the hand exhibits a marked and uncontrollable twist when passing over subterranean water, or mineral. The art was brought to Cornwall by merchant venturers in the days of Queen Elizabeth I, where it became known as dowsing, from an old Cornish word meaning to strike. The accuracy of the indications in the hands of an experienced dowser has long puzzled scientists, who ascribe the behaviour to a reflex action excited by some stimulus to the sub-conscious mind. We shall see that this is an over-simplification of a process of great significance.

For many purposes alternative forms of indicator are used, one of the more convenient being the pendulum, which can be employed for a wide range of investigation, including medical applications, as will be discussed shortly. The form of indicator is not important. It is simply a means of communicating with the true relationships existing in the real world. We shall see later that everything in the phenomenal world has its counterpart in the unmanifest realm, in the form of its eternally-existing time-body, which Jacob Boehme called the signature of all things; and it is with this real situation that the paranormal senses communicate.

This will be more easily understood if we first consider briefly some of the actual practices of dowsing, or radiesthesia as it is often called today. We are, in general, aware of the existence of the art, though many people regard it with suspicion. In any case it is usually considered to be somewhat remote from normal experience, best left to exponents of the occult. Such was my own reaction for many years. Yet it occurred to me after a time that if I really believed in the existence of the unmanifest world, subject to laws beyond the transitory evidence of the ordinary evidence of the ordinary senses, it should be possible to communicate with it practically, and not as a mere abstract speculation. So I began to experiment with the pendulum, which to my surprise provided increasingly intelligent responses. This was the more unexpected since I regarded myself as a normal down-to-earth individual. This confirms the belief that the paranormal senses can be used to a much greater extent than is generally recognised.

*   *   *

The dowser's pendulum comprises a small weight or bob on the end of a few inches of thread. If this is lightly held between the thumb and forefinger of the hand it will, in due course, begin to swing, sometimes in a simple to-and-fro oscillation, sometimes in a gyratory manner, either clockwise or anti-clockside. In the ordinary way this behaviour will be quite arbitrary, but if the operator has in mind some specific query, the mode of oscillation becomes significant and with practice can be interpreted accordingly.

If the pendulum is used in this manner it will provide clear answers to questions, provided these are themselves clear and specific. We shall give some practical examples shortly, but it must be understood that there is no particular magic in the pendulum itself, for it is only an indicator—my initial experiments used a cotton reel. Its movements are produced by involuntary muscular tremors, which are normally unco-ordinated, but can be directed by the paranormal senses *if they are so requested*.

Dr Nicoll often reminded us that the Universe is, by design, a structure of response to request. Scientific research is a process of formulating conjectural questions. If one does not obtain the expected answer, then the question is wrong, or inadequately framed. Indeed, all the amenities of modern civilisation which we take for granted are dependent on the expectation of a faithful response to suitably-formulated requests; and many of the experiences of life, which are often occasions of querulous complaint, are really responses to requests which we are quite unaware of having made.

The pendulum is a device for obtaining answers of a different kind connected with *relationships* in the Universe, which we have seen to be the province of the paranormal senses. The most significant aspect of pendulum dowsing, however, lies not in the results which can be achieved—and in the hands of an expert these can be quite astonishing—but in its use as a link between two different orders of intelligence.

Extra-sensory perception, of whatever form, must not be regarded as something divorced from life activity, but rather as an expansion of the limited awareness of the physical senses. Both are necessary to the understanding of the phenomena *as a whole*. This very realisation awakens the mind from its habitual slumber and creates new associations which are by no means confined to the exercise of dowsing.

*　　*　　*

Nevertheless it is of interest to consider some trivial illustrations of the way in which a pendulum can provide indications of relationships which are not apparent to the orthodox senses. For example, if I hold my pendulum over a 2p coin it begins to gyrate (for me, anti-clockwise). If some twelve inches away I place a second 2p coin, which we can call the reference sample, and touch it with my other hand the pendulum ceases to gyrate and goes into an oscillation towards the second coin, which I can interpret as indicating that both coins are of similar metal. However, if I use for the reference sample, or 'witness', a steel object such as a pocket knife, the pendulum will not change its mode, indicating that the materials are not the same.

However, if I use a so-called 'silver' coin (e.g. a 5p piece) as a witness, the pendulum will again swing towards it, suggesting that the materials are the same, which is clearly not true. Why has the pendulum given an apparently wrong indication? Actually, this is an example of loose questioning because, in fact, both coins contain a predominance of copper, and to this extent are similar. But if I ask specifically 'are these coins of *identical* material', the pendulum will say 'no'.

Now my scientific background tells me that coins, in general, are made from alloys of various elements. Hence if I use a selection of different metals as witnesses, the pendulum will confirm that the 'copper' coin is really bronze, which is an alloy of copper and zinc, while the 'silver' coin is actually made of cupro-nickel. Moreover, by using the pendulum in association with a graduated chart it can indicate the actual percentage of each constituent element in materials of unknown composition. For example, I once used this technique to test a foreign coin, which gave me 65 per cent copper and 25 per cent zinc, leaving 10 per cent unaccounted for. By using a succession of other witnesses I found that the missing element was aluminium.

These simple examples have been cited by way of illustration. It will be clear, however, that this kind of interrogation can only provide meaningful responses in relation to an adequate background of the subject under investigation. This is indeed a fundamental requirement of dowsing, particularly in its more sophisticated applications such as medicine, for without a thorough background of orthodox knowledge of the given subject, it is impossible to frame intelligent questions.

Hence the procedure has been described in brief detail merely to illustrate the way in which the pendulum can answer questions, provided these are clear and precise. The technique can be used in many ways. On one occasion my wife had been prescribed some unspecified tablets which I suspected might contain barbiturates to which she is allergic. By using a known barbiturate as a reference I was able to confirm my suspicion, and obtained an alternative medicament.

The pendulum, indeed, can be used to determine the suitability not only of drugs but of many familiar foods. To do this it is allowed to gyrate over a sample of the substance and the free hand is then interposed between the two. If the food is good the gyration increases in amplitude. If it is harmful the gyration is replaced by an oscillation, or in severe cases by a rotation in the opposite direction. Many allergies can be disclosed in this way more readily than by conventional methods which are apt to be laborious.

This is again by way of example, though it may be noted that there are in modern prepared foods certain energies which are inimical to the human organism. It is not a matter of chemical interaction, but of a subtle form of energy to which we will refer later.

The most remarkable aspect of the pendulum, however, is its ability to operate by remote association. This is employed in what is known as map dowsing, in which an examination is made of a map or plan of a particular area which is believed to contain certain possibilities such as subterranean water, oil or metal ores. By passing the pendulum over the map and at the same time asking the appropriate questions, an indication of possible sites can be obtained. These can be further pin-pointed on a larger-scale map, and finally verified by examination of the actual site, perhaps with an alternative form of detector such as a divining rod which may be more convenient in the open.

This map divining is used with surprising accuracy to locate archaeological remains, such as Roman villas, while the Abbé Mermet cites a number of examples of its use to locate missing persons. The significant feature of the technique is that it works, even though one may not understand why. Later, we shall suggest possible explanations.

A similar technique is used in medical dowsing which is beginning to be accepted as a valid method of treating previously intractable illnesses. Here the examination is conducted on a convenient sample, such as a blood-spot, from which a diagnosis can be made and treatment prescribed without ever seeing the patient, who may even reside at the other end of the earth. This is completely inexplicable to sense-based reasoning, but can be understood in terms of communication with the unmanifest counterpart in the noumenal world.

It is unnecessary to pursue these techniques in detail. Their significance lies in their illustration of the way that the paranormal senses augment, rather than replace, the response of the ordinary senses, which thereby become generally more alert as I have found from experience.

*   *   *

It must not be thought that dowsing is the only, or indeed a necessary, use of extra-sensory perception. It has been discussed at some length because it provides a basis for a practical understanding of the possibilities of the paranormal senses, which exist to provide communication with the real world. They are directed by the emotional part of the mind which in its pure state is concerned with relationships, as distinct from the sequential reasoning of the logical mind. As such they respond to impressions of a different quality from those of the physical senses.

As was said earlier, science is beginning to realise that the world of the senses is a chimaera, a partial and largely illusory portrayal of a more comprehensive reality. This realisation is prompting the postulation of concepts which not so long ago would have been regarded as utterly fanciful. One such idea of recent times has resulted from the discovery by astronomers of so-called 'black holes' in the universe. These are regions in space where the remains of a once giant star appear to have vanished altogether from the universe. The matter in the star, once many times more massive than our sun, appears to have been subjected to such colossal gravitational forces that it has been literally 'crushed out of existence'.

This has certainly set the cat among the pigeons, and to account for it the suggestion has been made that while the matter has ceased to exist in that part of space, it has moved *into another universe*. Professor John A. Wheeler, of Princeton, one of the world's most distinguished physicists, calls this other universe Superspace. He suggests that Superspace exists eternally and is the fabric from which the present universe was created and to which it will ultimately return, to be replaced by a new universe which will not necessarily obey the same laws.

Here is an admission of the possibility of a superior world behind the phenomenal appearance. It is still couched in terms of sense-based reasoning, and thereby fails to acknowledge that any such super universe will be animated by an intelligence and consciousness of an incommensurably higher order. To this extent it is an example of the upside-down thinking to which we referred in Chapter 4, wherein we showed that real truth is not merely an extension of ordinary knowledge, but is of an entirely different quality.

What is, for us, the real world is a pattern of relationships which is not manifest to the ordinary senses, but which contains the causes of all phenomenal behaviour. In Gurdjieff's Ray of Creation it is called World 24, or the Planetary World. In Theosophical parlance it is called the etheric world, a term which in some respects is more intelligible to conventional thinking. We have seen that a large proportion of physical phenomena involve what are called electro-magnetic waves, of which a small selection is manifest as visible light, but which actually extend over a vast spectrum of invisible radiations from brain rhythms to cosmic rays. In physical terms, any wave motion requires a medium through which it can be transmitted, but the 19th-century scientists were unable to discover any physical evidence of such a medium. They therefore postulated the existence of an all-pervading fluid, which they called the ether, in which these waves could travel.

This was later superseded by the mathematical concept of a 'space-time continuum', but this is really only a difference of terminology, and the idea of the ether is beginning to find favour again as a property of a tentatively-acknowledged etheric world. This accords with the concept of 'superspace', though the term is a misnomer because the etheric world is not a material entity. It should be regarded rather as a kind of force-field, a pattern of unmanifest possibilities which are progressively actualised in time by a transit of consciousness.

There is no reason why this transit should create only those manifestations which are detected by the physical senses. It is equally possible to envisage the simultaneous creation of other influences beyond the range of the ordinary senses, but to which the paranormal senses respond. These would produce the observed effects of extra-sensory perception and dowsing. This must be understood emotionally, because by its very nature the idea can only by tentatively formulated in words.

Something of the sort was suggested over one hundred years ago by the distinguished German chemist, Karl von Reichenbach, who believed that the Universe was permeated by a variety of non-physical vibrations of an entirely different character to electromagnetic waves. He therefore, in 1861, postulated the existence of another kind of all-pervading fluid, which he called *odyle*, as a vehicle for the transmission of these vibrations, which he suggested were responsible not only for the undefined 'sixth sense', but also for the maintenance of the vital energies of the body. His ideas were ridiculed at the time, though today they are beginning to receive some acceptance, albeit in different terminology.

In the light of the suggestions made above, we can envisage that Reichenbach's odyle and the ether of the physicist are one and the same, being simply the etheric force-field of the real world through which the interplay of different influences creates simultaneously the physical manifestations detected by the ordinary senses, and the 'odic' phenomena to which the paranormal senses respond.

*　　*　　*

Now it is in this etheric world that the real causes and situations lie. We can more easily understand this in practical terms by introducing the concept of *time-body*. This is discussed more fully in Chapters 8 and 9, which deal with the understanding of time, but it will be helpful to examine here the broad basis of the idea.

We are accustomed to interpret everything in terms of the present moment in time, so that life is a succession of events proceeding inexorably from the past to the future. Previous events belong to the limbo of the past, accessible only to a somewhat unreliable memory, while the future is yet to come. We shall see in Chapter 8 that this is one of the illusions of the senses, which by their very nature can only interpret impressions in sequence. We should really regard every object and event as the appearance at the present moment of something which has a continuing existence. The rose which I see out of my window was still a rose yesterday, or a month or year ago, and will still be in the future. Its appearance will change with its development, but it is an object which has a long body extending over many years of passing time.

Every object thus possesses its own time-body, of which the familiar appearance is merely a momentary interpretation, and this time-body exists permanently within the etheric world. The ordinary senses can only recognise its successive appearances in time, but the higher levels of the mind, which are not subject to these limitations, can comprehend the whole entity, and its relationship to any other time-bodies with which it is associated. The paranormal senses, which are directed by the emotional mind, can thus make contact with any part of the time-body, and although in their normal undeveloped condition the contact is tenuous, it becomes with practice increasingly complete.

In these terms one can understand the rapport which can exist between the emotional mind and any object or situation. It does not necessarily involve dowsing, though this is a valuable approach. Many people possess unusually good intuitive faculties which can be exercised without artificial aids by the cultivation of a quiet mind. In either case, the paranormal senses establish a communication between the time-body of the object under examination and that of the operator, or other person involved.

Furthermore, one can begin to understand the possibility of the remote awareness which is quite incomprehensible to the logical mind. It must be remembered that the time-body of any object or situation includes all its history and associations. The pattern of the etheric world is a fabric of interwoven threads extending up to (and beyond) the present time. Hence a map will have associations with the original site, even though it is apparently remote from it, and can serve as a focus for the mind of the dowser whereby his paranormal senses can establish communication with the object of his search.

Similarly, in medical dowsing a blood spot or other sample serves as a link with the individual from whom it was taken, because the time-body of the sample intersects that of the patient. Given adequate medical knowledge, the dowser can then assess the condition of the patient's time-body *at any part of its span*. This is why the same blood spot serves indefinitely. It does not itself change in some mysterious way to keep pace with the patient's development, nor are repeated samples necessary. Once the link has been established, communication can be maintained irrespective of the lapse of time or the separations of space.

It is impracticable here to discuss the medical applications of radiesthesia in detail. I have, in fact, dealt with them more extensively in my book on *Psionic Medicine* (Routledge). It is relevant, however, to note that the technique is based on the assessment by the paranormal senses of derangements in the vital energies which sustain the body—what Reichenbach called the *vis occulta*. Over 150 years ago Samuel Hahnemann suggested that all major bodily ailments were the result of disturbances of the vital energy pattern in the etheric world, which he called miasms, and that the remedy lay not in treatment of the symptoms, but in the restoration of the vital harmony. He further suggested that certain simple substances contained in themselves energies which could restore the balance. Even more strangely, he found that effective treatment could be provided by very small doses of substances which in a healthy person could actually produce the illness in question. This reinforced his belief that the real value of the medicaments did not depend on their chemical constitution but was derived from their subtle energy content.

This is the basis of homoeopathy, which is an accepted technique, though not widely used, mainly because its application is essentially dependent on the intuition of the practitioner. The development of radiesthesia, however, has made possible the scientific use of the paranormal faculties to locate and treat the aberrations of the vital energy with precise and sometimes spectacular results.

It will be evident from what has already been said that these energies are not physical, but operate within the paranormal or 'odic' realm. As a corollary, it can be understood that every substance contains its quota of this intangible energy, which may be beneficial or inimical to the human organism, as is well known in the sphere of naturopathy. Specifically, there are certain chemical elements which are not present naturally in the body which can produce malevolent effects.

One of the chief offenders in this respect is aluminium which is very widely employed in utensils used for cooking, and in the preparation of the extensive variety of packaged foods in popular use. The energy in this material is absorbed by the food in question, particularly under the influence of heat, and is then ingested by the body. It is not a matter of chemical interaction, but of odic energy, and can result in a slow poisoning of the system.

There are some who regard this very seriously, maintaining that it is responsible for much ill health today. This we cannot discuss here, but it may be noted that many allergies are the result of inimical influences which are not, as is commonly supposed, of a chemical origin. I have found from personal experience that, without being fastidious, my pendulum will often indicate the desirability of avoiding certain food or drink *for the time being*. As said earlier, one's bodily conditions change, and in minor respects the wisdom of the body, which far outstrips the ordinary intelligence, is well able to maintain a proper balance.

CHAPTER EIGHT

CONSCIOUSNESS AND INTELLIGENCE

We have made a number of references to consciousness, which is a faculty we take for granted, believing that we possess it as of right. Yet what do we mean by consciousness? It is usually deemed to imply being in full possession of one's faculties, as distinct from occasions when these are in abeyance, as in sleep or as a result of some accidental derangement. But the word means, literally, 'knowing all together' and hence implies, quite simply, awareness of what *is*. This awareness can obviously exist at different levels.

I once saw a television programme in which the camera had been linked to a microscope directed on to a sample of pond water, disclosing an organism called a water flea, invisible to the naked eye, pulsating with vigorous life. This produced a momentary realisation that this kind of activity was taking place in numerous ponds in my immediate vicinity, without any awareness on my part. I mentioned this to Dr Nicoll who said, "Yes, you make a very poor God, don't you!"

Evidently consciousness is utterly different from knowledge. We can learn a great deal about the fascinating phenomena of the physical world without being aware of more than the tiny fraction to which our attention is directed at any given moment. Even our personal behaviour is not accompanied by any appreciable awareness. I am at this moment giving my attention to the choice of the words to express the ideas I wish to convey, but all sorts of other things are also happening. My fingers are writing the words. Another part of the machine is smoking a pipe. My eyes and all my other senses are conveying impressions of my surroundings; and all this is being sustained by the unobtrusive operation of my normal bodily functions such as breathing, circulation of the blood, etc. I am unaware of any of this, my attention being fully occupied with thinking. Yet I believe myself to be fully conscious.

You may say that this is quibbling; that one may, and perhaps should, know about these many ancillary activities, but that it is necessary to concentrate on what one is doing, and not be diverted by academic distractions. This is merely a confession of the poverty of our so-called consciousness. It is possible to be aware of all these activities *simultaneously* with the performance of the immediate requirement. This would constitute a small expansion of consciousness, yet even this would be quite negligible by comparison with an awareness of everything that was happening in the physical world, let alone the real world.

Clearly the 'consciousness' of which we speak so glibly is a mere figment of imagination. Our understanding is still further restricted by our self-centred attitudes which create the belief that, as with our ideas of the mind, consciousness is the sole prerogative of man. This is a pathetically parochial view. Each world order in the hierarchy of the Universe possesses its own consciousness. The phenomenal world has a comprehensive awareness of the laws and conditions of its level, in conformity with which its many manifestations are produced. However, the noumenal world, from which these manifestations are derived, is clearly animated by an incommensurably higher order of consciousness, embodying relatively infinite possibilities and subject to less laws. Its awareness of *what is*, and the possible situations, is of an incomparably different quality.

Now man, as an inhabitant of the physical world, is necessarily subject to the direction of the phenomenal level of consciousness. This is of considerable magnitude, not by any means to be despised. It directs a remarkable intelligence which, however, is entirely circumscribed by the laws of its level and hence is mechanical in its operations (which include the patterns of behaviour of humanity as a whole).

Individual man, however, is equipped to respond to the direction of higher levels of consciousness, which provide the assistance necessary for his true evolution. We shall see, though, that to make contact with these levels a certain kind of attention is required. If this is merely perfunctory, a man's experiences are directed simply by the cosmic consciousness of the phenomenal world, which maintains the disinterested and automatic transit of ordinary life.

*   *   *

Ouspensky speaks of four states of (individual) consciousness. The first is *physical sleep* during which the mind receives the minimum of direction necessary to maintain life. Instinctive Centre continues to function, but the other Centres are quiescent. Hence the experiences have the relatively unreal, and innocuous quality which we call dreams.

The second state is the so-called *waking state* in which the voluntary Centres are operative, and impressions are translated into action by the varied programmes laid down in the brain. It embraces the first state, but contains the additional dimension of action and is thereby much more dangerous.

Our lives are normally lived entirely in these two states, which are both states of psychological sleep, not directed by any appreciable individual consciousness. There can be a transition from one to the other, but this is an automatic process directed by Instinctive Centre.

The third state of consciousness, called *Self Remembering* or Self Awareness, again involves an additional dimension. It embraces the two lower states but includes a range of higher possibilities, and is thus of discontinuous quality. In this state we can be aware of the full truth about ourselves, including the understanding of the translating mechanisms which relate us to the external *and internal* worlds.

Ouspensky said that we sometimes touch this state in moments of emotional shock, or when we find ourselves in an unexpected place. This produces, without thought, the feeling of 'inhabiting' the situation. But such experiences are transient; we have to try to achieve this state for ourselves, at first briefly but with persistence more consistently by the effort of metanoia.

The fourth state, called *Objective Consciousness*, embraces all the three lower states, and is concerned with the understanding of the *noumenal* world. It can only be attained by the operation of the highest levels of the mind, which are only accessible when a substantial measure of self-remembering has been achieved, but with which momentary contact can exist, often in dreams. This is explained in the next chapter.

* * *

Consciousness is not the same as intelligence. The word intelligence is derived from the Latin *inter lego*, meaning to read between, or in relationship to. Hence while consciousness will include the knowledge of all the possibilities in a particular field, intelligence is concerned with the manner in which any selected possibility can be actualised within the framework of the relevant laws and conditions. This is the function of the mind, which at any given level is the instrument of the consciousness of that level.

Now, incredibly, it never occurs to us that the mind requires nourishment. Yet this must be so, for all the activities of the Universe require energy for their operation. Each level, in fact, requires its appropriate food, which is derived primarily from energies coming down the Ray of Creation. This is a concept of the utmost practical importance.

Consciousness itself is not an energy, but is a force permeating the whole structure of the Universe, being the Divine principle by which the hierarchy is inspired. To translate this into action, movement is necessary (as is discussed in the next chapter). This is provided by the transit of consciousness through each of the levels, thereby producing the manifestations of the level below. This movement creates energy, so that each World Order has its own supply of Conscious Energy, which thus exists at different levels; and it is this which nourishes the appropriate minds.

However, for this to happen the mind itself has to be in a receptive condition, which involves two requirements. First, it must already possess some internal energy of a suitable quality, and secondly, it has then to provide a connection between the two. The internal energy is created by a fascinating process of transformation which is discussed in Chapter 12, while the connection is provided by *attention*.

In the state of psychological sleep in which we normally exist, the internal energy is squandered in the constant interplay of negative emotions and other wrong psychic functions. We are virtually unaware of the real self, so that we go through the day in a state of zero attention.

This waste of energy must be checked, so that there is at least a small reserve which can be used for attention. New ideas, or artistic appreciation, can produce a certain measure of *attracted attention*, which can provide fleeting contacts with individual consciousness; but if this is to endure it is necessary to cultivate *directed* attention which requires continued effort to transcend the limitations of habitual attitudes.

We shall see later that the body creates its own internal energies, by the digestion of the foods which it eats. These energies are of progressively higher quality, but do not *automatically* reach the level of conscious energy. Hence the organism has to draw its quota of this precious energy from the cosmic pool. This reliance on cosmic good-will is clearly indicated in the familiar Lord's Prayer, which contains the phrase, 'Give us this day our daily bread'. As is so often the case, the translation is inadequate, for the word 'daily' is, in the Greek, epi-ousios, which means 'for the purpose of what is one's own'. Hence the request is not for physical food, but is a plea for the continued availability of the necessary conscious energy. It has always seemed to me that this very request, so mechanically repeated, should be accompanied by a grateful acknowledgment of the enormous debt we owe to the Universe, something which is normally taken as a right.

The debt is, indeed, explicitly mentioned in the next phrase, inadequately translated as 'forgive us our trespasses as we forgive them that trespass against us'. The wording in the original is altogether more significant, a better translation being 'Cancel our debts *to the extent* that we cancel what we are owed'. This indicates clearly that if we can cancel what we imagine we are owed by other people, or by life in general, we may thereby make at least a partial payment for what we have been given.

*   *   *

Now, since the logical mind necessarily thinks in terms of comparisons, we tend to believe that a higher level of consciousness can only be attained by forsaking the old. This is quite wrong because the higher *embraces* the lower. The ordinary level of consciousness relates us adequately (and necessarily) to the events of life; but a higher level of consciousness can create an expanded awareness *simultaneously* with the habitual response.

This is possible because of the more rapid speed of operation of higher levels. Any perception requires a certain quantum of energy, which takes a certain time to accumulate (as we shall discuss later). It is quite small, being about 100 microseconds with ordinary perception, but the more rapid time-scale of Emotional Centre enables it to register impressions in a mere fraction of this time, so that it sees a thousand connections where the ordinary mind sees only one.

Hence, in a moment of self-remembering, everything becomes much more vivid. There is a quality of 'seeing all together' far too rapid to express in words, so that one has a feeling of actually belonging to a vastly expanded and living Universe. Dr Nicoll once said that it was as if things knew that they could come out of hiding, and go on playing. I can remember idly watching a spider and suddenly becoming aware of its meaning and, it seemed, that of the Universe itself. The inspiration, of course, was purely transient, and I can recollect only the incident and not the understanding.

These brief (and irrelevant) moments are in the nature of gifts and cannot be contrived. Any change of state can only occur when a sufficient *quantity* of energy has been accumulated. One has to persist in the effort of self-remembering; then there may be a sudden transition producing a brief flash of greater awareness. This, however, will not endure, for it is really a morsel of food for a higher level, and is eaten thereby. This is the refinement of the ore of which we spoke at the outset, and is a continuing requirement.

Hence we are not suddenly translated to a permanent state of increased consciousness, but we begin to experience moments of awareness which accompany the necessary daily activities. One experiences with increasing frequency the feeling of 'inhabiting' the situation, of looking out on the phenomenal world through the mechanisms of the body; and this creates a new awareness which does have a certain permanence.

It is important to understand the idea that a higher level of consciousness *includes* the more detailed manifestations of the lower level, all of which have their place and purpose. If my house catches fire, it would be stupid to indulge in a dispassionate analysis of my reactions. I must take immediate steps to cope with the emergency in the most practical manner available. But all this activity can be *accompanied* by an objective awareness of the whole situation, which is present without 'taking thought'.

We have, in fact, the ability to respond to higher levels of intelligence simultaneously with the necessary attendance upon life; so that we can begin to 'maintain two separate days', one within the other.

CHAPTER NINE

THE NATURE OF TIME

One of the more elusive aspects of existence is its dependence on time. We readily adapt ourselves to the conditions of space, which is consistent in its behaviour. Time is more wayward. It does not flow at a uniform rate; some experiences are over all too quickly, while others drag on interminably. In a moment of crisis everything happens very slowly, though the experience may only last a few seconds, and there are many other oddities which we accept as a matter of course.

It is a subject which has attracted the attention of many philosophers. My own interest was aroused by Dunne's 'Experiment with Time', later reinforced by the ideas of Ouspensky and Nicoll, as a result of which I was able to rationalise many aspects of the behaviour of this strange phenomenon, and believed that I thereby understood it. Actually it can only be properly comprehended with emotional thinking, since it is part of the structure of the noumenal world. Its behaviour at the phenomenal level is merely a manifestation of conditions of a higher order.

Indeed, when we speak of time in the ordinary way we are really referring to the operation of our *time-sense*, which is an acquired faculty, just as much as the other translations of the senses which we take for granted. To a small child, yesterday and tomorrow have no meaning. It lives entirely in the moment, but gradually comes to recognise a certain sequence in events from which it develops a time-sense necessary for a satisfactory relationship to life.

Our normal awareness of time, in fact, is entirely subjective. The successive events of life are translated by this time sense, which has been developed by experience as part of the programming of the brain, and operates mainly unconsciously. Yet this very translation is multiple in character. Part is concerned with the recognition of the cosmic sequence of hours and days, over which we have virtually no control (though modern high-speed flight can do curious things to our clocks). Yet within this framework the changing events are translated by a personal time-sense which can operate at widely differing rates. This we know from experience, and can even control to a small extent without necessarily understanding the process.

* * *

Plato likened our situation to that of a man living in a darkened cave, to whom the world outside is exposed through a narrow moving slit; so that he has no concept of the real world as a whole but is only aware of its transitory appearances through the moving slit. This is entirely in accord with the idea that we live in a world of illusion, a portrayal through a restricted range of senses of a much greater, but unmanifest, real world. Now, however, the idea is reinforced by the realisation that this portrayal is the result of some kind of transit through the real world.

What is this transit? It is, quite simply, a transit of consciousness. We can envisage that the conditions which exist (eternally) in the real world are actualised by an awareness which is not static but moves through the region, creating the illusion of time. This is an idea which is mentioned in broad terms in Plato's Timaeus Myth, which deals with the Creation. This, he says, comprises "that Substance which is undivided and always the same, that which cometh into being and is divided into bodies, and . . . a third sort of substance in the middle between the same and the other". This will be recognised as an exposition of the Law of Three; but he goes on to say : "But since the pattern, which is eternal, could not be joined to any created thing, God

made an image of Eternity progressing according to number—
to wit, Time."*

If we now relate this to the concept of the hierarchy of levels
in the Universe, we can see that, as was suggested in the previous
chapter, each level is enlivened by the transit of an appropriate
order of consciousness which creates the manifestations of the
level below. But because the levels are incommensurable, each
level will have its own time scale, any one of which is virtually
infinite in terms of that of the succeeding level. Specifically, this
means that the level which is for us the real world operates with
a time scale which on our level is *eternal*. So that everything
exists permanently in the real world, but (some of) its possibilities
are actualised in succession by the transit of phenomenal consciousness. (We may note here the proper meaning of eternity,
which is not an indefinite extension in ordinary time but a condition existing at a superior level.)

It is the transit of consciousness through this already-existing
region which creates the events and structure of life. This is not
an inflexible transit, though, because it can be undertaken by
different levels of consciousness, each creating different patterns
of events. The basic transit is produced by an impersonal level of
consciousness which is concerned only with the creation of events
of historical significance. This dictates the activities of the phenomenal world, partly in respect of its physical characteristics and
the processes of evolution, and partly in respect of the manifestations of human behaviour which determine the course of
history.

The physical body of man is subject to the same laws, but his
psychological behaviour can be directed by different levels of
consciousness to which he has access, and these can produce
different transits through the domain of Eternity. This could
create a completely different life, but is more usually concerned
with different paths between situations created by the cosmic
transit.

To understand this it is necessary to distinguish between

* J. A. Stewart, *The Myths of Plato*, Macmillan, 1905 (now out
of print).

happenings and events. A happening is a conjunction of physical circumstances, whereas an event includes all the psychological reactions which arise. These are enormously complex, involving not only one's own reactions but those of a host of other people who are *or have been* involved in the situation. An event is thus vastly greater than a happening, and since reactions can be of widely differing quality, it is evident that there can be many paths between the same sequence of happenings.

This is an idea which one must develop for oneself. It entirely alters the quality of one's relationships with other people, and particularly one's memories of previous experiences. By way of example, suppose I receive a letter accusing me of incompetence in some recent activities. It is from a man whom I dislike and mistrust, believing that he is plotting my downfall. I indulge in a welter of internal considering, justification, offended pride, anxiety and so forth, with which I become completely obsessed. My wife becomes involved in this miasma so that I treat her as a thing of no account. I make an appointment to meet this detestable character in two days time, until when no useful negotiation can begin; but instead of dismissing the matter until then, I prolong the event internally in a tumultuous fret at the delay.

These reactions are entirely imaginary, quite divorced from the actual situation, which is determined by the impersonal transit of events in cosmic time. So that the transit of my individual consciousness, such as it is, between the two happenings—the receipt of the letter and the subsequent interview—has taken a long and devious path through quite unnecessarily unpleasant territory.

An objective assessment might show that the accusation had some element of truth. Moreover, it could permit me to see myself through the eyes of my accuser, and to see that my behaviour *inevitably* produces in him the antagonism which poisons our relationship. The whole event is changed for both of us, irrespective of the outcome. He may still succeed in accomplishing my downfall, but it will not matter in the same way. My internal transit between the two happenings will have taken a path through a region of different (and superior) possibilities, and will have done so with much less expenditure of energy.

This example is by no means abnormal. It is typical of the way in which we meet life situations of all kinds. But it serves to show how, in actual practice, the transit of *individual* consciousness can take widely differing paths through the real world, even though the sequence of happenings may be unaltered.

*   *   *

Many philosophies of time attempt to explain it in mathematical terms, involving some mysterious 'fourth dimension'. This is unfortunate since it places undue emphasis on what is really only an incidental aspect of the subject. We saw earlier that a dimension is, by definition, merely a framework for the measurement of extension of any kind. The succession of events involves an extension which cannot be measured in any of the three dimensions of space, but takes place in some entirely different direction which *includes* their manifestation in space. A simple line can only be produced by the movement of a point in time, and in fact all the familiar objects which our senses detect are extensions in space which either are or have been created by movement in time.

We do not ordinarily see things in this way because it is not necessary. Our relationship to the external world is adequately maintained by a three-dimensional interpretation of the impressions received by the senses, and the brain is programmed accordingly. But if we are to make a proper use of our faculties we have to create new associations which do not take everything for granted. I once was momentarily aware of a blade of grass as something actually coming into being 'before my very eyes'. This awareness produced a flash of insight (not contrived, nor repeatable).

We can, therefore, understand emotionally the existence of a region in which consciousness moves in paths which are not measurable in terms of space but in an additional dimension. The significant characteristic of this superior region is that it contains

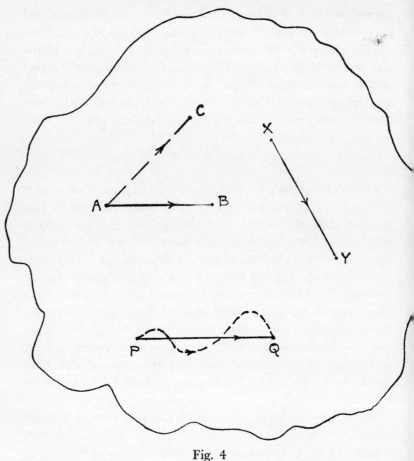

Fig. 4

Illustrating the Possibility of Different Transits through the Domain of Eternity

a further degree of freedom, permitting the exercise of different possibilities. This was illustrated by the philosopher C. H. Hinton, who postulated an imaginary race of 'flatlanders' living entirely in a surface. Their world would include the dimensions of length and breadth, to which they would adapt themselves completely, but they would have no concept of depth. Let us imagine, for example, a population existing in the surface of a bowl of water.

An object such as a finger introduced into the water would produce in the surface a shape having a form and movement which, to them, would be an arbitrary and inexplicable phenomenon, involving inconvenience and possibly destruction to many. Yet to the owner of the finger, possessing the superior awareness of depth, there would be no mystery in the operation, which would have some purpose.

By analogy we can conceive that the real world contains additional degrees of freedom which do not exist at the phenomenal level. We can illustrate this further by another, even simpler analogy: Let us envisage the real world as a surface, on which patterns may be drawn with a pencil, as in Fig. 4. The pencil point represents consciousness which by its movement creates lines which represent events. This process can evidently happen in many ways.

It can move, for instance, from A to B; or from A to C. It can move through some other region which would create a pattern of events in a different part of time, as at XY. It can move at varying speeds. Finally, we can have two pencils, which might make the transit between the same two points by different routes, as shown at PQ; and there could be many pencils in use simultaneously.

This is a very simple analogy, but it serves to illustrate the possibility of different transits of consciousness through the same region. The horizontal line PQ in the figure could represent the transit of 'clock time' between two happenings—a transit produced by the cosmic and impersonal intelligence of the phenomenal world. The dotted line represents the transit of individual consciousness which has actualised entirely different possibilities within the same transit of cosmic time.

* * *

Analogies like this do not 'explain' time, though they can help to develop new associations which awaken the more emotional parts of the mind to an understanding of real relationships. And with this more emotional thinking we can begin to appreciate one of the most puzzling aspects of time, namely pre-cognition.

This usually occurs in dreams, of which there are many authentic examples. One in my own experience occurred while I was still at school. I dreamed that my mother had written to ask if I could have special leave to attend a Pachmann concert. I had no knowledge of Pachmann, apart from having heard his name mentioned by a casual acquaintance some months previously, and certainly knew nothing of any forthcoming concert. I even forgot the dream until I was summoned the next day to an interview with the housemaster which, to my surprise, went exactly as I had dreamed.

Many people have had similar experiences. Moreover there are instances of quite impersonal foreknowledge. J. W. Dunne records a dream of a fire in a Mediterranean liner, in which he was in no way concerned, but which happened some days later. This experience prompted his investigations into the subject. Experiences of pre-cognition are, in fact, much more common than is popularly supposed. Though usually regarded as abnormal, they are really the natural exercise of our true functions.

We have seen that the deeper, but normally dormant levels of the mind respond to higher orders of consciousness, and these are not circumscribed by the limitations of the ordinary level. This means that they can move within the real world (wherein everything exists eternally) both in the future and in the past. However, the brain is not normally equipped to translate the information which they provide, being directed only by sense-based programmes (including the acquired time-sense). It is therefore confused, and in fact rejects the information.

During sleep the ordinary sense-based programmes are partly quiescent so that there is a possibility of response to superior levels of consciousness which can transit 'future' possibilities. These are extensions of the present line of time and will be actualised in due course, provided that the present conditions continue. However, these may change in the interim, so that the actual future may be different. But in any case the brain has not been properly programmed, so that it presents a garbled mixture of past and future events, often in incorrect location and the wrong order.

Ordinary dreams do not even have this significance because the normal emotional and intellectual minds are *not* quiescent. We take our worries to bed with us so that the brain is still fed with (internal) life impressions. Nicoll often said that we should go to sleep with 'a rose on our heart', wiping the slate clean of all the events of the day. If this can be done the brain is released from much useless activity and can respond more easily to superior influences, even though it may not be able to interpret them.

In such a situation one's dreams can be significant, often containing elements of real truth. Ouspensky called these 'dreams from Higher Centres', meaning that they are translations provided in response to programmes directed by a higher level of the Universe. One such dream from my own experience may be quoted by way of illustration. I live in a bungalow, but one night I dreamed that I was taken outside and shown a complete, but unfamiliar second storey. This was a way of telling me that I was living mainly in the lowest levels of my Being and that there was a fully formed but uninhabited level available for exploration.

If we pursue this idea further it will become clear that communication with higher levels need not be restricted to dreams. The brain can be released during working hours from a great deal of the unnecessary activity which results from the host of spurious internal impressions derived from life. This permits it to respond to impressions provided by the paranormal senses mentioned earlier, creating not only new understanding but the appearance of the faculties of clairvoyance and prophecy.

* * *

The understanding of time clearly involves the use of fresh associations beyond the conventional interpretations of the senses. These one has to develop individually by examining for oneself the various possibilities. While one has necessarily to start with intellectual thinking it is important to avoid being distracted by attempts to arrive at tidy explanations. We have to begin to *feel* the nature of time which expands our understanding of the real relationships in the Universe.

We can start quite practically by realising the extent to which we are imprisoned by the conventional time-sense. The figures on the clock are usually meaningful only in relation to our plans for the day, and clock time can be singularly unaccommodating in this respect! There is no need to be the slave of these self-imposed programmes which are simply part of the panoply of personal desires. As one begins to substitute alternative programmes based on a different scale of values, significant moments can be expanded and unpleasant experiences squeezed up and discarded. One can indeed take a different course through the noumenal world, which by the very act creates experiences of a superior quality.

CHAPTER TEN

CHANGING THE PAST

There is an aspect of time which is of the greatest significance in the pursuit of the real adventure. It was said in the previous chapter that everything exists eternally in the noumenal world and that the successive events of our normal experience are only brought into being by the transit of consciousness through this real region.

Now this is not really difficult to understand if we are willing to stretch our minds. Suppose I make a journey to a neighbouring locality. On the way a variety of objects will come into being before my eyes and will disappear as I continue on my way. The environment and buildings of my destination will grow miraculously from nothing as I approach, and when I leave these will disappear. Yet I do not believe that they were all created as I made the journey, or that they no longer exist after I have gone.

Similarly, all the objects and events of the phenomenal world are brought into being by a transit of consciousness. They are the appearances in passing time of unmanifest causes in the noumenal world which exist both before and after the passage of the particular consciousness involved in their display.

In particular, all the incidents and experiences of my own life are manifestations of a pattern of possibilities which continues to exist in the noumenal world. This is called my *time-body*, and belongs to me permanently, even though the physical experiences derived from it are swallowed up in the 'past'. It is within this time-body that the real adventure lies, but this requires a quality of awareness beyond the conventional associations of ordinary memory and to appreciate it we should first examine briefly the remarkable mechanisms of the normal memory.

*　　*　　*

Ordinary memory is of two types. One is concerned with the retention of knowledge or skills acquired during the course of experience. This is achieved by the creation, by trial and error, of a pattern of associations which, once established, will provide the required action whenever the particular skill is required. The second form is more elaborate and is concerned with the recollection of previous events and experiences. This is much less reliable, in practice, being usually inaccurate and often failing altogether.

Actually, both forms of memory utilise the same basic mechanism, which operates in a fascinating manner. It used to be thought that every event in one's experience was stored in the brain, but this is now known to be neither correct, nor even practicable. A simple analogy is that of an automatic telephone exchange. Every time a call is dialled certain equipment is brought into use, but if this remained permanently connected, the system would very quickly become saturated, and unable to accept any more calls. Hence, once the required connection has been established, the apparatus is cleared for further use. Similarly, an incoming 'call' to the brain sets up the appropriate connections in its network of associations and, having produced the required response, clears its circuits in readiness for further information.

Now these operations are performed by a vast assembly of groups of nerve cells called neurones. These are elaborately interconnected in such a way that a given item of information supplied by the senses sends electric currents through the network, so producing the appropriate response. In the process there is a small change in the structure of the individual nerve cells which pre-disposes them to react in the same way to any similar information received subsequently. This is the way associations are formed by experience, which quickly become stereotyped, and create what we call memory.

Within this pattern, however, is the important element of

meaning, to which all incoming impressions are related. This is itself a complex sub-network which may be relatively simple but can be very sophisticated. Unless it has been activated, the memory train is incomplete and no action results.

With instinctive and simple voluntary activities the meaning is clear, and consistent action results. The general run of events, however, involves a wide variety of meanings. We have seen that the impressions of any events are translated through a series of *personal* sub-programmes, which have a certain meaning. Any subsequent experience having a similar element of meaning can re-activate the original pattern, producing a partial re-experience of the earlier event (but not, of course, a complete repetition, because that part of the pattern which involves 'clock' time is not the same). But personal meaning is *not* consistent. Meanings change as experience develops, certain elements being emphasised while others are diminished in importance. Hence, when one recollects some event in the past, only those aspects of meaning which correspond with the present conditions are operative, so that the memory is coloured to our own advantage. Memories which elude us can be re-awakened if we can find the missing element of meaning; but if the original event had no significant meaning for us we cannot remember it at all.

Meaning, in fact, constitutes an important part of our psychology. Not only does it change from time to time, but it is usually very limited in scope. One of the most important aspects of metanoia is the creation of new meanings.

This is a necessarily very abbreviated review of a highly sophisticated mechanism, involving some 10,000 million nerve cells, but it suffices to illustrate the broad principles of the operation. It shows that events are *not* permanently recorded in the brain, and that ordinary memory arises merely from a certain pre-disposition in the intricate circuitry which can be re-activated by similarities of meaning. Moreover, it is an operation involving a purely mechanical level of consciousness, which ceases with the death of the physical body (and even during life if the mechanism is deranged).

*   *   *

In addition to this perishable memory, however, there is true memory, which does not reside in the brain, but exists in the noumenal world. This we have seen to be a region of eternally-existing possibilities, *some* of which are actualised by the transit of appropriate consciousnesses. Now we can envisage that just as some of the cells in the brain are activated by an actual event, so any possibility in the noumenal pattern which is actualised by a transit of consciousness remains partially (though not irrevocably) activated. Hence the transit leaves a kind of trace in the real world, which remains in existence. This is the time-body, which is a permanent record of every experience in the life. It does not disappear on the death of the physical body, but continues to exist in the domain of Eternity.

Here is real memory as distinct from the acquired but untrustworthy memory of ordinary experience. Swedenborg makes a similar division into what he calls exterior and interior memory. He says that while many things may be obliterated from exterior memory, the interior memory contains a complete record of experience and is, in fact, the 'book of life' which is said to be opened at death.

Now there is a very significant, and inspiring aspect of this concept of the time-body, which is that it can be modified. If I go for a walk through the countryside I can take many different paths. I may stick to the main road, but I may see more interesting territory to one side, perhaps on a higher level, and at an appropriate point can explore this different route. I might find that this led me on to an unsuspected field path and decide that if I come this way again I will try to follow this more attractive route from the beginning. There are, in fact, innumerable (though not unrestricted) possibilities.

There is a similar freedom of movement within the territory of the noumenal world, which has its hills and valleys, its high places and its swamps. The transit of consciousness through it can take many different paths. Moreover, the route can be changed at any time. It can avoid the muddy places and choose a cleaner path. We are necessarily talking in terms of analogy, but by inference one can understand that at any point in the time-body a different level of consciousness will actualise different possibilities within the eternal pattern, so that the time-body will be changed.

Our ordinary thinking will interpret this as applying only to the future, for one can appreciate that more conscious behaviour could alter the course of one's life. But the concept of time-body is of far deeper significance because, as just said, it can be modified at any point. This modification can include experiences which have been actualised in 'the past'. We have seen that the higher levels of consciousness (which we possess but do not normally use) have a certain freedom of movement within the real world, and can therefore re-activate any part of the time-body.

This idea can be interpreted in various ways. The theory of recurrence (which I will discuss later) suggests that the whole life can be lived again. But this implies that one has to wait for death in order to make a fresh start, whereas it is possible to make a much more immediate endeavour *now*. As just said, the higher levels of consciousness have a certain freedom of movement within the real world. Moreover, in any event more than one consciousness is involved. The 'happening' is created by the transit of cosmic consciousness (which creates 'clock' time), but the accompanying psychological manifestations are created by the transit of individual consciousness which actualises a range of associated possibilities in the noumenal world. The time-body contains at least two intertwined threads.

The individual thread can pass through different levels, and in fact it pursues a devious route, because even in the normal state the level of consciousness is not constant but is continually fluctuating. There are times when one is in the grip of anxiety or negative emotions, while at others one may be more detached and even have moments of self-remembering.

In a state of greater awareness the time-body begins to be seen as a whole, and it is then possible to smooth out some of the deviations in 'the past', and even create a path at a superior level. This can be done because the previously actuated possibilities are not irrevocably committed, and can be modified.

* * *

For some considerable time the idea of time-body is a purely academic concept. Yet if it is kept in mind it gradually leads to the development of a new *meaning*. For many years my own activities were concerned, quite rightly, with the pursuit of material success. There was a certain acknowledgment of spiritual values which I fostered through my interest in Freemasonry, and later by studying the ideas of Dr Nicoll's teaching. But all this was merely *added* to my existing philosophy, which still remained predominant.

There was, in fact, a certain inner conflict between material and spiritual meanings, which only resulted in the failure to respond adequately to either. I began to perceive that the real choice was of a different quality, since a superior level of awareness *embraces* the subordinate level. One can and should be whole-hearted in the performance of the necessary activities of life, but with a feeling of being an onlooker in the game.

There is actually a certain innate awareness of one's time-body which is normally distorted almost beyond recognition by the inaccurate, and even lying, recollections of ordinary memory. A more honest retrospect brings together different parts of the time-body in their true relationships, not connected on the thread of passing time. There is a change in the feeling of I, which no longer resides in the many false exercises of ambition and self-love and the resulting criticisms of oneself and others. These can be squeezed up and thrown away, while experiences which arise from a genuine, and almost impersonal, delight can be expanded in meaning.

In this way the whole life can gradually be transformed in quality, not by changing the events but by bringing them into awareness. This is the alchemy, for which there is plenty of material.

CHAPTER ELEVEN

THE PLACE OF MAN

An important aspect of meaning is that of man himself. Despite his arrogant conceit he would appear to be of very minor importance within the stupendous intelligence of the Universe. This is certainly true as long as he remains asleep in the comfortable belief in some mythical hereafter. However, esoteric teaching says that he has a significant purpose, but one which can only be fulfilled when he understands his place in the structure. Only then can he recognise his true potentialities.

To this end we must examine further the hierarchy called the Ray of Creation, which was shown in Chapter 4 to comprise a succession of world orders of increasing complexity. We saw later, however, that these manifestations require energy for their operation, so that the structure has to be enlivened by the transmission of forces through the successive stages, which generate energies of progressively coarser quality. The system is then replenished by the return of these energies through appropriate refinements at each level, so that there is a rhythmic flow and return of energy—the 'breath of Brahma' mentioned earlier.

This rhythm, however, cannot develop properly unless the successive levels are themselves in a suitable condition to accept the relevant energies. Hence they do not exist in a haphazard sequence but conform to a curious pattern of harmony controlled by the second of the two fundamental laws in the Universe—the Law of Seven, which we must discuss briefly.

*   *   *

We are accustomed to think of progress as continuous and uniform. Actually this is not so, even in ordinary life, and the Law of Seven states that any real development proceeds in a succession of *discrete* steps, each representing a specific degree of actualisation. There are seven such intervals, producing a structure having eight steps, which is called an *octave*, the first and last stages being of similar character but different intensity or quality.

However, these intervals are not uniform, for the octave contains two places where the progress is restricted. The pattern can be represented by the notes of the (major) musical octave which, in Tonic Sol-fa notation, forms the scale Do, Re, Mi, Fa, Sol, La, Si, Do' (which is said to have been devised by the mediaeval monk Guido d'Arezzo to illustrate the sequence).

Now the notes of a musical octave are produced by sound waves of a gradually increasing rate of vibration, with the upper Do having exactly twice the rate of the lower. This produces a sound of the same quality but differing in pitch. A uniform progression would then be achieved if the vibration rates of the successive notes increased by approximately 8 per cent per step. But this does not produce a harmonious relationship between the notes, which can only be obtained by arranging that the successive vibration rates are simple fractional multiples of the lower Do. The relationships in the octave are thus :

	Do	Re	Mi	Fa	Sol	La	Si	Do'
Relative vibration rate	1	9/8	5/4	4/3	3/2	5/3	15/8	2
Interval (Percentage increase)		12·5	11	6·5	12·5	11	12·5	6·5

It will be seen that while the vibration rates are simple fractions, the intervals between them, i.e. the relative increases in rate, are not uniform. Five of the intervals are roughly the same, corresponding to a full tone, but there are two places,

between Mi and Fa, and between Si and Do', where the increase
is only half the normal, producing what is called a semi-tone.

These two semi-tones are places where the rhythm has changed.
They arise from the overall pattern of harmony within the scale
and are thus not merely abitrary. The arrangement, in fact, is a
representation of the manner in which all the progressive manifestations in the Universe develop in accordance with this octave
structure, in which there are two places where the impetus
weakens. These are called points of shock (or sometimes places of
missing semi-tone) and if the octave is to proceed, some reinforcement is necessary at these places. The transmission of energy
throughout the Universe is accomplished through a harmonious
assembly of octave patterns, great and small, intersecting one
another at appropriate places to provide the necessary shocks,
constituting what in ancient terminology was called 'the music of
the spheres'.

*   *   *

We do not normally recognise the influence of these octave
patterns, though they operate throughout the Universe at all
levels. They are of two types. All creative processes develop
through *descending* octaves, in which the original intention is
implemented in a succession of increasingly detailed stages. Alternatively, there are *ascending* octaves, directed by the integrating
forces in the Universe, which provide successive refinements of
quality.

Neither type will develop properly unless it is correctly
reinforced at the appropriate points of shock, and this technique
we do not normally understand. Hence as a preliminary to the
consideration of the Grand Design, let us discuss a very small, but
quite practical example, namely the construction of a table. This
starts with the (unmanifest) idea which, if the intention is strong
enough, will be translated into detailed plans. These plans, however, have then to be turned into hardware, requiring actual
materials and the tools and skill to use them. If these are not
available, the octave will peter out. We could, by way of illustration, suggest an octave pattern as overleaf :

	Do′	Idea of table	
Shock (Decision to proceed)	☐		
	Si	All possible forms of table	
	La	Particular type of table	Unmanifest thought
	Sol	Specific requirements	
	Fa	Detailed design	
Shock (Materials, tools and skill)	☐		
	Mi	Preparation of materials	
	Re	Fabrication	Physical form
	Do	Actual finished table	

This is a trivial example which nevertheless illustrates the discontinuity inherent in genuine progress. Each stage must be completed before the next can start, and at a certain point a reinforcement is required from something outside the octave (but of appropriate quality) if the process is to be completed. The culmination is a manifestation of the original intention in more specific but less intelligent form. (Clearly the physical table in the example cannot itself design further tables).

This octave pattern operates in many subtle, and usually unsuspected ways. Life indeed is full of 'broken' octaves which fail to be completed because of the absence of the necessary shocks, though we often recognise this need without knowing why. We learn by experience to wait for the right moment before proceeding; or we set a project aside temporarily and attend to something quite different, which often provides the requisite shock. But all this is only a small part of the hierarchy of creation, which is a structure of interwoven octaves of enormous profusion and scale.

In addition to these creative octaves there are the integrating octaves in which the energy passes in the reverse direction. Such octaves start from the *lower* Do, which is not animated by intention, but by submission to a higher level. This octave proceeds by a succession of transformations of quality, from coarser to finer. The existence of these octaves is even less generally recognised, but they are an essential part of the mechanism of energy-return in the structure of the Universe, in which there is a vast pattern of transformation, continually operating on many scales and levels. A typical example, which we normally take for granted, is the process of digestion in the body. This not only produces physical refinement of the food but transforms it into the psychic energies of thought and feeling.

We will discuss this idea of transformation more fully in the next chapter, but we may note here that the essential feature of an ascending octave is that it involves the ascent of an already-created ladder. The process requires re-inforcement at the appropriate points of shock but, if successfully completed, culminates in a manifestation of the initial concept at a superior and more intelligent level.

*　　*　　*

The supreme example of a creative process is the Universe itself. Since this is a harmonious structure, the successive stages of manifestation must conform to the Law of Seven. Hence the world-orders in the Ray of Creation will constitute the notes of a descending octave, as shown in Fig. 5. It will be seen that the planetary level is at the note Fa, while the phenomenal world is at the note Mi. Between these notes there is a missing semi-tone, which means that the forces coming down the Ray cannot proceed without the reinforcement of an external shock.

This is provided in the cosmic structure by a *side octave* which starts at the level of the Sun (World 12). The note Si in this side octave corresponds with the planetary level, after which the notes La, Sol, Fa pass through the place of the missing semi-tone in the main octave. This reinforcement enables the forces to proceed through the notes Mi and Re of the phenomenal world, culminating in the lower Do which represents a condition of lifelessness

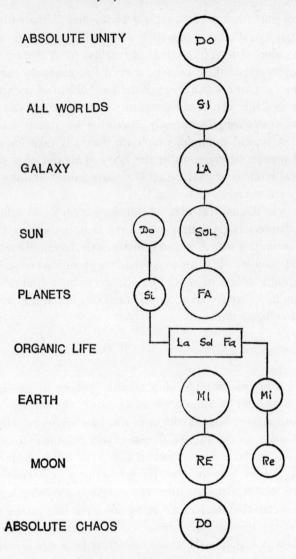

Fig. 5
The Great Octave

sometimes called Absolute Chaos. It could be regarded as the 'other side' of the Absolute Creator in a Universe which is itself the Deity and forms a closed structure enlivened by the forces circulating through it.

The detailed implications of this main octave, however, are beyond the scale of human intelligence which operates entirely within the side octave, and even so, only to a limited extent. The side octave, in fact, is a structure of considerable intelligence which serves as a vehicle for the transmission of energy across the Fa–Mi gap in the main octave, and its return in modified form by the processes of transformation.

The notes La, Sol, Fa of this side octave correspond with the phenomenon of Organic Life, which plays an essential part in the life of the Earth. It receives energy from the (physical) Sun which it absorbs and retains, creating in the process an atmosphere which traps the heat but cuts off certain vibrations which are inimical to life. Without this absorbent film the energy could not be retained and certain essential transformations in the structure could not take place. Life, in fact, did not appear on the earth by accident, but was created by a higher intelligence for a specific purpose.

However, this is only part of the functions of the side octave, which is concerned with the transmission of a wide range of influences involved in the cosmic pattern of return to the Source.

*　　*　　*

It is within this side octave that man appears. His physical body is part of Organic Life, but he is designed to occupy the whole octave. He contains materials of all the levels represented by the successive notes, but those at the upper end are not fully developed. These he has to nourish by transforming the quality of the lower materials in which he normally has his being. If this is done it provides a special kind of energy return, appreciably more rapid than that produced by the normal cosmic process.

Man's true meaning is thus of much deeper significance than

is apparent in life terms. He is an incomplete creation but is equipped with the possibility of completion by a particular kind of individual effort. However, this has to be of an *impersonal* quality, inspired by the influence of the immeasurably superior intelligence of the Sun level, which is, for us, Divine.

This is very different from the pursuit of personal advancement. As we shall see in the next chapter, it involves saving some of the energy which is normally squandered in the spurious activities of self-importance. This energy can then be used to nourish the more real levels in the structure, but only if it is suitably transformed in quality and cleansed of the poison of self-love.

We find this difficult because the hynotism of life causes us to translate everything in terms of personal satisfaction, so providing many comfortable, but quite erroneous interpretations. For example, in a discussion on scale with his disciples, Christ says, "Are not two sparrows sold for a farthing? And not one of them shall fall to the ground without your Father" (Matthew 10, 29). This is conventionally interpreted as indicating that every smallest event in the phenomenal world is personally supervised by a benevolent Deity. But in fact the phrase 'without your Father' has the implication of *awareness*, for the word translated as 'without' is a derivative of the word for mind. The real meaning of the statement is that all these happenings are 'within the mind' of God. A higher level of consciousness is not concerned with a stupendously detailed knowledge of the activities of a lower level, but understands and sustains its operations.

The simple truth is that God—which for us is the Intelligence of the Sun level—is not aware of us individually. This is only possible if we can transform our level of being, as discussed in the next chapter. The influences from the Divine level, however, are continually operating through the medium of subordinate angels, for whom we may have some individual existence. The Chinese philosophy of The Golden Flower postulates that groups of people (of similar spiritual stature) are in the care of their own guardian angel.

Even so, no communication can exist as long as we are asleep, disguised in the sombre trappings of the self-love which are not visible to a higher level. I once wrote a story about an apprentice angel who was told to assist a group of earthlings. After a week he had to confess complete failure, telling his master in some bewilderment that he just could not see them! We have to find (and pay for) psychological clothing of a more luminous character.

CHAPTER TWELVE

THE NOURISHMENT OF
THE UNIVERSE

In the automatic succession of days and years it rarely occurs to us to wonder what sustains the Universe. We assume in a vague way that it must contain some source of energy, but are not very concerned as to where it comes from. Yet since the Universe is a living structure it must eat—a very strange idea to our ordinary way of thinking.

Now, eating is basically a process of transformation. In physical terms, we take food into the stomach where it is transformed by successive refinements into the non-physical energies of thought and feeling. Similar operations take place throughout the Universe, which is a vast structure of transformation on many different scales whereby the energy expended in the successive created processes is returned to the Source. Each level is designed to produce refinements of the available energy which serve to nourish the level above, while the residues or waste products of the process provide energy of a suitable quality for the level below. This is the mechanism of energy transfer throughout the structure. It was expressed by the 14th century mystic, Meister Eckhart, in one of his discourses wherein he says: "All the work and waste of Heaven is caught midway in the sink of Earth."

Gurdjieff said that the place and purpose of everything in the Universe could be assessed in terms of what it eats and what it is eaten by. This applies equally to ourselves, though the idea of being eaten by something higher does not penetrate our customary arrogance. I recall an amusing broadcast play by Lord Dunsany

117

called The Use of Man, which opens with a discussion among a number of hunting types about the use of various creatures. They give patronising approval to the many creatures which man has enslaved, including the faithful horse and dog, and they all agree, amid much laughter, that the one completely useless creature is the mosquito. Later that night one of the party has a dream in which he is called to the bar of judgement and is told that mankind has been deemed to be a failure and that unless he can find a creature who can speak in its defence, it will be destroyed. He does not take this very seriously, for surely all the animals to whom he has 'been kind' will speak in his favour; but one and all they reject him, until at the last minute the small voice of the mosquito is heard, saying, "I will speak for man; he is my beautiful *food*!"

A typical Dunsany whimsy, yet with an undercurrent of seriousness, for in a Universe where nothing is wasted, man will be food for something. At death his body feeds the Earth, but his experiences serve a different purpose. They are designed to nourish beings of a very high level (which Ouspensky called Archangels). The greed and violence of sleeping humanity, however, is quite unacceptable to such beings, and in fact can only feed subhuman levels.

* * *

Let us consider this idea more deeply. It will be evident that since the various levels in the Universe are discontinuous, transformation is not a matter of mere increase but involves a change of state. A simple example is the boiling of water in a kettle. The heating at first merely causes a slight increase in volume; but the water still remains water until sufficient energy has been absorbed for the molecules to change their state and become a gas—i.e. steam.

The steam is at a higher energy level than the water and possesses greater possibilities. It can, for example, drive a steam engine. But this change of level can only occur (abruptly) when the water has accumulated a sufficient *quantity* of heat. This has important psychological implications, since it shows that in attempting to achieve a change of level a certain persistence is required in order to accumulate the necessary quantum of energy; moreover, such energy as has been acquired must be preserved and not allowed to become dissipated.

There are many other examples of transformation, as distinct from mere change. Consider, for instance, the life-cycle of a butterfly: it starts with an egg which develops into a caterpillar; this feeds on the material at hand, and grows until, at a certain stage, it wraps itself in a cocoon, from which in due course it emerges in completely different form as a butterfly. This is a transformation, for the world of the butterfly contains new and superior possibilities quite beyond the experience of the caterpillar, one of which is the faculty of reproduction. It is interesting to note that the eggs laid by the butterfly do not produce butterflies but *caterpillars*, which are transformed at the appropriate time into butterflies. The seed has to be sown and develop at a lower level of existence until, if it survives, it is ready for transformation.

Man is in an identical situation, though on a greater scale. He is a seed sown from a higher level into the phenomenal world. In it he has to develop according to the laws of that level until he reaches a stage at which transformation into his real condition is possible. But the transformation here is *not* physical (and certainly not something which happens automatically after death). It is a psychological transformation for which he has to prepare himself during his transit through the phenomenal world.

This is the task. The ultimate aim is to re-ascend the ladder of the side octave and so attain unity with the Divine level. This would be a transformation into a being of entirely different quality and one which would not need to inhabit the earth. This, however, requires many lives and the immediate and practical aim during the present life is to provide what nourishment we can for the higher levels within us, by transforming the quality of the energies involved in our ordinary experience.

*   *   *

119

We do not ordinarily think of experience in terms of energy. Yet every activity involves energy, which takes many forms. Scientifically, matter and energy are interchangeable, and we are familiar with many processes of exchange, such as the conversion of chemical energy into electrical form in a battery, or the translation of mechanical to electrical power in a dynamo. But these are exchanges at the same level, whereas transformation, by definition, involves a change of quality.

We have to understand that the Universe is a structure of energy levels which are of discontinuous quality. Within the limited region which we inhabit there are four distinct levels of energy, namely mechanical, vital, psychic and conscious. Mechanical energy is the energy of physical movement, whether in the body or the physical world as a whole. Vital energy is the energy of life, which is of a higher order. No mere increase of mechanical energy will produce vital energy, while the psychic energies of thought and feeling are of a still higher order, and can moreover exist at several distinct levels. Hence the quality of any experience is not determined only by the happening, but depends on the psychological energy content, which can be changed.

To understand this better, let us consider a process of transformation which we normally take completely for granted, namely the nourishment of the body. We take in physical food which is automatically and miraculously transformed in the organism, firstly to supply the physical replenishment of the cells, and by still further transformations, to create the vital and psychic energies by which we live, think and feel.

Ordinary physiology regards these processes as mere energy interchanges, but actually they are discontinuous changes of *quality*, which can only be produced by the influence of a higher level. Hence the process involves a succession of discrete stages involving the ascent of an already-created octave structure, as illustrated in Fig. 6. The operation commences with the intake of physical food, which constitutes the Do of the (ascending) octave. This is taken into the stomach where, by the action of ferments already present in the organism, it is transformed into a pulp called chyme, which constitutes the note Re.

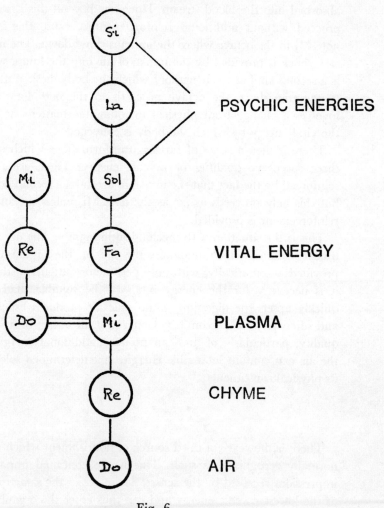

Fig. 6
The Food Octave

It is then still further refined into substances capable of being absorbed into the blood stream. However, beyond this it cannot proceed without additional reinforcement, because this is the note Mi in the octave where the impetus slows down. The necessary shock is provided by the intake of air into the lungs, which is a second kind of food (without which the body dies). With this (automatic) shock the octave proceeds to the note Fa, which involves a change from physical to intangible matter—actually the vital energy by which the body is enlivened.

There is then a series of further transformations which create three successive qualities of psychic energy. These are partly reinforced by the fact that the intake of air starts a second octave, but this only proceeds as far as the note Mi, unless yet another reinforcement is provided.

This is the situation with mechanical humanity. The necessary transformations which maintain the life of the organism are provided automatically, with only perfunctory attention, though it is necessary for the energy intake to be suitable. Bad food quickly upsets the digestion, while stale air produces listlessness and often physical discomfort. Conversely an intake of a better quality, particularly of air, can produce additional energy, for the air can contain intangible energies not determined solely by its physical constituents.

*　　*　　*

There is, however, a third source of nourishment which is not normally recognised as such. This is the continual impact of impressions received by the senses. These are of the same quality as the lowest psychic energy and can thus enter the organism at this point. But to be effective they have to be digested. Physical food can only be transformed by digestion in the stomach. Air can provide no nourishment until it is accepted and used by the lungs. Similarly, impressions have to be transformed in a kind of psychological stomach *which we have to develop*.

It is the transformation of impressions which constitutes the real alchemy. When we are very young everything is new and fresh, so that this rich food of impressions is really taken in. But we are educated by 'our betters' to suppress the sense of wonder and to take everything for granted. The energy of impressions becomes squandered in the stereotyped acceptances of habit, and ceases to be transformed to any appreciable extent.

By stretching one's thinking beyond the habitual interpretations, the mind can be enlivened by energies of a superior quality. The impressions are taken in clean, and unadulterated by habitual associations, and this starts a new octave of psychic energies, as shown in Fig. 7; moreover, this provides the necessary shock to

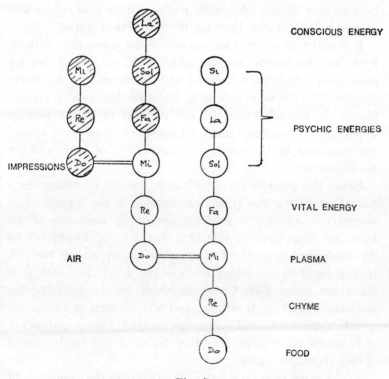

Fig. 7

Illustrating Additional Energies created by Conscious Intake of Impressions

the air octave, which progresses to an extent able to provide a small amount of conscious energy.

This operation, however, requires conscious direction, which in the ordinary way is lacking. We are, indeed, normally unaware of the vital importance of this third food. We appreciate vaguely that repetition of the same kind of activity makes us jaded, so that we continually seek new experiences in an instinctive thirst for fresh impressions. It is well known that the recovery of invalids is noticeably assisted by cheerful news, gay flowers, etc. Conversely, there are people who live almost entirely on a diet of self-pity or remorse. They are most unpleasant to live with because they do not adequately reinforce their vital energy and so steal it from others. They are the vampires of legend.

It is said that whereas we can survive for many days without food, and for several minutes without air, we cannot live for more than a fraction of a second without impressions. Evidently therefore there is some automatic intake of this essential energy, but in the normal course the vast majority of the impressions impinging on the senses many thousands of times every second are translated by the stereotyped associations of habit and are not digested.

Hence this precious energy is largely wasted. To make even a partial use of the true possibilities existing in the organism it is necessary to develop a gradually increasing awareness of the incoming impressions, so that they do not automatically fall on the established network of conventional interpretation but can be translated by the higher levels of the mind. The exercise is sometimes called First Conscious Shock (as distinct from the automatic shock of breathing) and will be seen to produce a greatly augmented supply of psychic energies; moreover these are of increased potentiality, since they are at or near the beginning of their respective octaves.

At the same time, it is necessary to exercise discrimination in the intake of impressions, for, just as bad food or air can poison the system, so the psychic energies can be impaired by bad psychological food. To some extent, impressions are neutral, their influence being determined by the translations made by the brain.

124

But there are impressions which are indigestible and cannot be transformed—impressions which excite feelings of morbid curiosity, horror, ill-will, etc. These we have to spit out, otherwise they may cause distressing psychological vomiting.

It is evident that the exercise of First Conscious Shock is essential to the development of our real capabilities. It does not involve reasoning so much as an emotional appreciation of the different translations which are possible. This is not a once-for-all operation, but has to be a rhythmic process similar to the physical act of breathing, though at a much more rapid rate, as we shall see in the next chapter. However, for the greater part of the day we do not exercise our spiritual lungs at all.

CHAPTER THIRTEEN

THE ALREADY-EXISTING PATTERN

In his biography of Michelangelo, *The Agony and the Ecstasy*, Irving Stone mentions the difficulties which the sculptor encountered in finding suitable blocks of marble for his intended statues. He would spend weeks patiently visiting quarries until he found a slab which contained *within itself* the figure he had in mind. His work then consisted of chipping away the stone to reveal the already-existing truth.

This notion of 'already-existingness', which has been spoken of earlier, is one which I find of great depth. It conveys the idea of fulfilment of an intelligent pattern which is taking place *now*. There is in my garden a small juniper tree which has grown over the years within a characteristically compact form. It does not spread like a fruit tree, but knows from its code that it has to grow upwards. It is in the process of filling a space which has already been prepared for it.

Ideas of this kind can only be understood by the emotional mind, which can recognise the existence of levels of intelligence and time scales of a different order. Yet such concepts are apt to be of an abstract quality, whereas we have to try to bring them within the range of experience. One of the ways of achieving this is to consider some of the relationships between the different rhythms in the Universe.

We have seen that the nourishment of the organism (and of the whole Universe) depends upon appropriate transformations of energy. Because any change of state requires a certain quantum

127

of energy, the process is essentially rhythmic. This is readily understandable in respect of the act of breathing, for we inhale fresh air and exhale carbon dioxide and other waste products at regular intervals of approximately 3 seconds.

Physical food is eaten, and the waste products excreted in what is, overall, a daily rhythm occupying 24 hours, which is roughly 30,000 times slower than the time of breath. On the other hand, impressions are of a much briefer duration, but one which is nevertheless finite. It was said that a certain time is required to acquire a sufficient quantum of energy, and for physical impressions this is of the order of 1/10,000 of a second. Any phenomenon of shorter duration than this is not registered by the senses. Hence the intake of impressions is also a rhythmic process, occurring 10,000 times a second—that is 30,000 times quicker than the air rhythm.

Now this is no mere coincidence, because this curious factor of 30,000 is a measure of the relationships between the time-scales of different levels of intelligence in the Universe. The successive levels of creation create appropriate patterns of manifestation, each of which constitutes an independent *cosmos*, obeying the same fundamental laws, but on a decreasing scale, as was indicated in the ancient Hermetic saying "As above, so below"; and each has its own time-scale, of decreasing order related by this factor of 30,000.*

Let us apply this to our immediate environment. Each cosmos is a living structure which has its own characteristic time of breath. We have seen that for man this is 3 seconds. However he is a unit in the larger cosmos of Organic Life, which has a different time scale. Plants, for example, absorb carbon dioxide from the air during the day and return it at night, and natural

---

* This is not an arbitrary figure, but is derived from a mathematical relationship, due to Minkowsky, which says that a moment of time t in a given world order is equivalent to a time jct in a world of a higher dimension, where c is the velocity of light and j $(= \sqrt{-1})$ is a factor denoting a change of dimension, which we can disregard numerically. If we take the moment of time as 1/10,000 sec. and multiply this by the velocity of light, which is 300 million metres/sec., we obtain the factor 30,000.

rhythms in general are controlled by the alternations of light and darkness; so that the time of breath of Organic Life is 24 hours, which is 30,000 times longer than that of man.

At the same time, man is himself a structure of cells. These constitute a smaller, but highly intelligent cosmos which provides a remarkably efficient service, and clearly has a more rapid time-scale. For example, a glass of brandy produces an almost instantaneous feeling of warmth; yet this involves a whole series of elaborate chemical transformations occupying several hours of cellular time. Temporary repairs to damaged tissue can be effected in a few minutes, yet they involve operations which in our time would take days. All of this is consistent with a time scale 30,000 times quicker than that of man. In fact, cells are known to breathe by a continual interchange of gases, which may well occur rhythmically some 10,000 times a second.

We can therefore understand that we exist within a structure of (at least) three cosmoses, and that the rhythm of our essential nourishment corresponds with the time of breath of these cosmoses, as :

Cosmos	Time of breath	Significance for man
Organic Life	24 hours	Physical food
Man	3 secs.	Air
Cellular World	1/10,000 sec.	Sensory impressions

The range of cosmoses extends both above and below this group. For example, two stages higher is the cosmos of the Sun level in which the time of quickest impression is 80 years, so that at this level the whole life of a man is barely perceptible; while below are the atomic and electronic cosmoses which are equally beyond the scale of sensory perception. These need not be listed in detail, the significant cosmoses being those within the range of normal experience. In a moment of self-remembering one can sometimes feel oneself to be actually a part of Organic Life; or one may be aware of the cells of the body pursuing their appointed functions.

* * *

E

This difference of time scale in the various levels of the universe helps our understanding in many ways. It shows how a higher level can be aware virtually instantaneously of events which follow one another in sequence at a lower level. This applies particularly to the levels within our own structure. We saw in the last chapter that there are three separate levels of psychic energy (which nourish the three levels of the ordinary Centres). Each of these has its own time scale, increasing by a factor of 30,000 at each level.

This is the reason why the emotional levels of the mind see in a flash solutions which elude the ponderous processes of reason. The classic example of this is the experience of the mathematician Sir William Hamilton, who is said to have seen the solution to a hitherto intractable type of equation called a quaternion while walking across a bridge in Dublin. All of us have these occasional moments of insight which are really a normal exercise of our latent faculties.

We have seen that the proper working of the organism requires the transformation of impressions. Yet this cannot be done by the ordinary level of the mind, which works with the same speed as the impressions themselves. It is necessary to be aware of the impressions through the emotional mind which, because of its higher speed, can see the 'dumb blonde' making all the wrong connections and can provide alternative programmes which will produce more real translations. This creates a kind of impersonal delight which is very acceptable to higher levels. I recall that Dr Nicoll once said that to be eaten by an angel was a moment of bliss.

If these deeper levels of the mind can be awakened, they begin to respond to the emotional impressions detected by the paranormal senses, for which the 'quantum time' is 30,000 times less than is required for normal perception; which is why in a moment of self-remembering one sees thousands of connections instead of just one.

It is evident that we normally make very indifferent use of our faculties. There is a further aspect which is even less appreciated. Since the intake of impressions is a rhythmic process it should be accompanied by the exhalation of the waste products of such transformation as has been achieved. What these are we do not ordinarily know, but they will clearly have the quality of the immediately-inferior level of energy, namely vital energy, so that for a moment everything will appear much more vivid. This, however, is a relatively infrequent occurrence. For much of the time we are spiritually constipated.

...accomplished by the Oklahoma is the wave pattern of such competition is distinctly curved. What does all we do this method. This method will place into the quality of the utilization of gathered of specimens by all...experiment for a manner, everything will appear there may been this. This however, is even more interesting to compare. Continued of the name is...

CHAPTER FOURTEEN

IN SEARCH OF MAGIC

An enduring recollection of my schooldays at Christ's Hospital is the Leaving Service held in the Chapel on the last day of term, at which by tradition was read the passage from St Paul's Epistle to the Philippians (4, 8) which runs :

'Finally, brethren, whatsoever things are true, whatsoever things are honourable, whatsoever things are just, whatsoever things are pure, whatsoever things are lovely, whatsoever things are of good report; if there be any virtue, and if there be any praise, think on these things.'

Now this is a passage having a quality of magic. It is no mere philosophy of expediency, but evokes a response from the emotional mind, creating an experience which can remain forever one's own. Real literature, and particularly the Scriptures, abounds with similarly magical phrases which impinge directly upon Essence and hence have a peculiar and abiding power.

We are not, of course, referring to the illusions of the stage magician, but to real magic which is conventionally associated with the idea of the supernatural and hence regarded with suspicion. Moreover, it is usually interpreted, following the formulations by Sir James Frazer in *The Golden Bough*, as the art of direct control (by man) of the forces of nature. Now while there are authentic instances of such control, particularly among the so-called uncivilised tribes mentioned in Chapter 7, this is a degradation of the truth, for magic is an art of much deeper significance.

A better understanding was shown by Dr R. R. Marett, who defined magic as the art of communicating with a supernatural power, or *mana*, which animates all things in the Universe. This has a much less personal connotation, and is consistent with the concept of the etheric force-field, with which we have seen that communication is possible through the paranormal senses. In this realm forces can operate by *conscious* direction of the higher levels of the mind. While these may, if appropriate, be applied for individual benefit, they are primarily concerned with cosmic harmony.

Magic is thus the manifestation of influences of a very high quality, which ought to be regarded with reverential awe and gratitude. One can then understand that certain words and phrases do indeed have magical properties, for they can stimulate the inner parts of the emotional mind. Further, because they have done so over the centuries they have become impregnated with the reverence of countless generations and so possess great power to awaken the spirit.

However, like everything else in the Universe, this has to be paid for. It is not sufficient to rest content in the emotional delight of the idea. Still less is there any virtue in 'vain repetitions' of supposedly magical slogans. I have on my desk a small card bearing a question mark (which often intrigues visitors). It is intended to remind me to ask myself repeatedly 'who am I?' or some similar question which can lift me briefly out of the morass of identification with life; but the symbol itself contains no intrinsic power. The magic only operates if I make the effort to respond—*now*, not when I have finished what I am doing.

Similarly with the moments of spiritual uplift which one experiences 'accidentally'. These have to be recognised as gifts from a higher level. This very acknowledgement is a form of payment, permitting the reception of further influences, not necessarily of the same kind, but of similar quality. These moments of understanding have to be preserved from profanation by material considerations, so that they can gradually be augmented until a sufficient quantity of energy is accumulated to permit a momentary change of state. This is the basis of real prayer, which is the attempt to communicate with higher levels, and in speaking of this to his disciples Christ emphasises the need for persistence.*

*   *   *

Magic does not operate solely through the medium of words. Art and music have similar power to awaken the emotional mind, and can likewise be impregnated with the worship of earlier generations. This, of course, only applies to real works; much of what passes for music today is intended merely to titivate the senses.

Actually the whole Universe is a magical structure, permeated at all its levels by the consciousness of the Absolute. Most of its operations are beyond the range of human comprehension, but we can respond to the immediately adjacent levels. We saw in the previous chapter that man is a denizen of the much larger structure of Organic Life, which has its own intelligence and consciousness. A part (but only a part) of its function is the provision of nourishment for mankind, not only as physical food but even more in the delicate impressions which impinge on the senses every moment. These favours are taken entirely for granted. As I write, my garden is a riot of colours and scents, which provide great pleasure. But in this perfunctory enjoyment there is no feeling of gratitude for these gifts, which are really quite beyond my puny contriving, though I have contributed in a small way to their nurture. It rarely occurs to me to say thank you to a rose for being what it is. Still less do I recognise it as a living being. Yet Sir Jagadis Bose, the eminent Indian plant physiologist, showed in 1906 that plants could feel, and modern research has established somewhat belatedly that they respond not only to actual physical contact but to the associated thoughts. A plant will cringe, just like a human, at the threat of damage, and conversely will respond to affection. So that the idea of talking to plants is no idle fancy.

Plants, in fact, know that they have a function to fulfil, either as food or in the creation of beauty. This they do the more

* Dr Nicoll discusses this at length in *The New Man*, Chapter 8 (Watkins).

135

willingly and with less pain if their efforts are acknowledged. This aspect of awareness is very well discussed by Carlos Castaneda in his book *Journey to Ixtlan* (Bodley Head).

What of the other denizens of Organic Life, for which vegetation provides both shelter and nourishment? There are the birds and the beasts which, being mobile, can more easily be regarded as individual beings. We may often be appreciative of the song of a bird or the beauty of its plumage, or take pleasure in the graceful movements of an animal. It rarely occurs to us to be grateful for these delights.

Insects do not rank as individuals in our estimation, though they may do to a child. I remember my small grandson picking up a woodlouse and saying to it, 'Hello, what's your name?' We have little appreciation of their use and tend to regard them as pests. Yet they have their place and purpose in the highly-intelligent pattern which we take entirely for granted.

We spoke earlier of the idea of compassion as a sharing of experience. If we can surmount even to a small extent our egregious preoccupation with ourselves we can begin to develop a compassion with Nature which has the quality of magic. For this sense of wonder and delight creates higher levels of meaning which are experienced *simultaneously* with the necessary meanings of ordinary life.

*   *   *

At the same time we can begin to develop an awareness of the cells of the body. As we saw in the previous chapter, these belong to their own cosmos, directed at their level by a remarkable intelligence, which again we take for granted. We give no thought to the intricate physiological activities which the body undertakes in our daily existence, such as the circulation of the blood, the interchange of gases in the lungs, the digestion of food involving elaborate chemistry performed with an astonishing simplicity and rapidity, the repair of tissues damaged by accident or disease, and a host of other activities of which we are normally unaware unless something goes wrong.

Even then we do not really understand the situation, but only the superficial symptoms which we attempt to alleviate by various palliatives, often clumsy and sometimes dangerous. The enlightened physician acknowledges the intelligence of the body and endeavours to assist it in effecting its own cures. It is, indeed, possible to communicate with this intelligence and listen to the cells, which in their specialised groups know all that is necessary about themselves. Ouspensky once said that if we could learn to listen to their conversations we should discover an entirely new basis of medicine.

This would clearly involve the exercise of a higher level of consciousness. We are not concerned here, though, with the medical aspects of the situation so much as with the possibility of achieving a greater awareness in the ordinary conditions of life. This becomes increasingly possible as we learn to acknowledge the subordinate cosmos of the cells, to which we actually stand in the relationship of gods—and by no means always benevolent gods.

We have seen that the average life of cells is only a day in our time. During this lifetime they go about their appointed tasks under the direction of Instinctive Centre and in a quite impersonal manner. They do what is required of them because this is their role. But one can envisage that if their work receives the approbation of what is for them a higher authority, their work will have a new quality of delight. In practical terms, this means that if we can cultivate an awareness of the cosmos of cells, the whole body is invigorated.

More usually, we are very querulous gods engulfing the cells in an aura of discontent, and are then surprised that we feel physically off colour. I remember Mrs Nicoll once saying that, having been a whole day in the grip of negative emotions, she realised that she had thereby condemned the cells of her body to a lifetime of hell!

With a more conscious attention it is possible to converse with different parts of the body and perhaps understand their problems. The old-fashioned remedy of a piece of flannel over an aching joint works not from any physical effect but because it is an

E*

137

expression of sympathy with the cells concerned. On one occasion I was distracted by acute sciatica during an important meeting, so I asked my leg if it could hold up its repairs for the time, and the pain immediately ceased. A more spectacular example is the case of a patient who was scheduled for a routine operation, which would be followed as a matter of course by special after-care. When the time came, however, the surgeon decided not to operate, but to go through the same after-care routine as if he had actually performed the operation. The patient made a complete recovery.

*　　*　　*

These are all ways of expanding one's awareness. They create a growing feeling of *inhabiting* the Universe of far greater majesty than the phenomenal world interpreted by the ordinary senses. One begins to see the events of life as part of a cosmic plan which is significant for man only to the extent that he can use the experiences as material for transformation.

The world today, despite its material advances, is still (and increasingly) governed by the violence and inhumanity which has characterised all recorded history. According to astrological lore we are in the Age of Kali-yuga, or barbarism, which has still a long way to run before being succeeded in the cosmic cycle by a new Golden Age. These are inescapable conditions, not to be rejected, but understood as the base material in a pattern of superior meaning.

It is the attainment of this understanding which is the real aim, and this is supported by the whole magic of the Universe—if one can learn how to use it. There is a passage in Isaiah (57, 15) which possesses for me great magic. It runs, 'Thus saith the high and lofty One that inhabiteth eternity, whose name is Holy: I dwell in the high and holy place with him also that is of a contrite and humble spirit'.

Here is the epitome of real aim; and its magic does not lie in the mere emotional delight of the idea, but in its power to stimulate the search for the holy place *in oneself*, inhabited by the I's of the spirit, which can begin to accompany the necessary activities of the lower self. This is contrition, which does not mean regret but implies assessment of scale, for the word comes from the Latin *conterro*, to grind to powder. The word humble is derived from a root meaning to put into the ground, implying the possibility of growth.

CHAPTER FIFTEEN

THE PHILOSOPHER'S STONE

We have been in search of the secret of the real adventure, in the course of which we have made a number of excursions into unfamiliar territory. We have discovered new ways of thinking which have created different associations, and as we begin to assemble these we find, to our surprise, that the coveted secret has apparently been in our possession all the time.

It is, of course, normally hidden behind the veils of complacency and habit, but as these are torn aside the truth is revealed. This is the secret. Yet the very simplicity of this discovery can mask its significance, for we mistake the clues for the reality. We continue to pursue fresh ideas, believing that these will, of themselves, accomplish our salvation, which is like wishing to visit the East and spending one's money buying tickets through various agencies without using any of them.

We have to make use of such understanding as we possess, for by this very act it will be increased. The ideas so far discussed can be developed in much greater detail, but this is of no value until one has begun to apply what one has already understood. Ideas, in fact, are no more than catalysts in the alchemy which we have to perform for ourselves, alchemy involving the transmutation of *existing* experience.

For many years I believed (secretly) that a diligent study of esoteric ideas would enable me to attain a demonstrably superior level of consciousness, and possibly emulate men like Nicoll or Ouspensky. Gradually I began to perceive that any such grandiose aim was quite unacceptable to a Higher Intelligence, and that my only real possibilities lay in the fulfilment of the life which had been allotted to me.

*   *   *

Reference was made earlier to the idea that the course of one's life is not entirely arbitrary but conforms to a pattern which is significantly appropriate to one's spiritual needs. It is an idea which is found in many philosophies, notably in Plato's myth of Er, the Pamphyllian soldier slain on the field of battle. When after ten days he is collected with the other corpses, however, he is found not to be dead. Whereupon he describes how his soul had gone up to a place where the mouths of Earth and Heaven are joined, with judges in between. There follows a description of purified souls drawing lots from the lap of Lachesis (the Past) and buying lives from the samples available. From this the wise chose lives best suited for their continued development. They then journeyed with their guardian angel to the plain of Lethe, where each was required to drink of the River of Forgetfulness before returning to Earth; whereof the unwise drank more than their measure, but the prudent limited themselves.

This contains the implication that the real part of a man, which we have called Essence, is required to visit the Earth to acquire food for its development. For this purpose it is permitted, according to its stature, to buy a life which will provide the best opportunities for the adventure. It is not allowed to remember the pattern completely, so that the development of the situations may appear to be far from advantageous from purely life considerations. Yet a trace of real memory tells us that they are meaningful, so that to waste one's energy in continual complaints or attempts to escape is simply unintelligent.

One can understand that this unmanifest pattern can be responsible for the apparently arbitrary turns of Fate which alter the course of our lives. I have already quoted examples in my own experience, and one is constantly encountering similar instances. Sir Geraint Evans once said in a television interview that he became a professional singer as a result of an accidental audition when he was serving in the Royal Air Force. This is 'the divinity that shapes our ends', which provides the opportunities beyond ordinary contriving.

These opportunities are not simply examples of good fortune. Indeed they may sometimes appear quite the opposite, for certain kinds of misfortune can be valuable material. They are part of the pattern of possibilities designed to facilitate the growth of Essence, which we have seen to be the real purpose of earthly existence. However, there is no compulsion in the matter. We may not accept the opportunities nor perhaps even recognise them. The concept of an allotted life does not imply a rigid predestination.

It contains, in fact, very considerable possibilities; but to appreciate this we must remind ourselves of the conditions in the real, but unmanifest world.

* * *

Because of the incommensurability of levels we can only speculate about the behaviour of the noumenal world, and this speculation must be in the simplest possible terms, for there is an axiom known as Occam's Razor, which says that the fewer the assumptions the greater the probability of truth. Hence we can start with the simple premise that man is a spiritual entity (called Essence) inhabiting a physical body. His real part resides within the unmanifest world which is a region of infinite possibilities, not subject to the laws of passing time, and hence, for us, *eternal*.

Now we saw in Chapter 9 that the appearances and events of the phenomenal world can be regarded as being produced by the transit of consciousness through the noumenal world, and that within this virtually infinite domain there are many transits of different kinds of consciousness. The transit of cosmic consciousness creates the illusion of passing time, and the multiplicity of objects and happenings of life, including the physical body in which Essence is clothed. The psychological behaviour of this body, however, is determined by the transit of individual consciousness, which can take an independent path through the region. It can move forwards or backwards, relative to cosmic time, and at its own speed, so that it possesses entirely different degrees of freedom.

This is a basically simple idea which *contains all the possibilities with which we need to concern ourselves.* We can envisage that during the transit of cosmic consciousness which we call life, individual consciousness can move freely through the 'past' and the 'future'. It could make repeated transits through the same life, or it could pass through some other region of time, in what is called reincarnation. Possibly several such transits can be made simultaneously. In any case, it is well known that consciousness can visit other parts of the region which have not yet been actualised by cosmic time, without necessarily inhabiting a different body, so producing prophetic vision.

These are, of course, matters of speculation which must be interpreted emotionally, because the real world cannot be 'explained' in logical terms, and attempts to do so only introduce unnecessary difficulties. There are, nevertheless, two aspects of the idea which are of practical significance.

The first is that Essence is immortal and continues to exist in the real world beyond the death of the physical body. What we call death is simply the cessation of the transit of individual consciousness through the particular part of cosmic time. So that Essence continues its quest in the unmanifest world towards unity with the Divine level. When anyone dies we should think of them as participants in a continuing adventure (in which, indeed, they may be hampered by over-emphasis of our personal sense of bereavement).

However, if this progress is to be significant it is important to ensure that Essence is *properly nourished* during the lifetime of the body. We said earlier that the whole object of the adventure called life was to promote growth of Essence. This requires the transmutation of the experiences provided, and if this is not done to a sufficient extent, Essence may be starved. Moreover, it can easily be poisoned by bad psychological food, such as a consistent diet of lies or blasphemy. It is said that lives which contain recurring tragedies are indicative of a dying Essence.

*   *   *

Now in terms of ordinary understanding it is evident that the full development of Essence can hardly be achieved in a single lifetime. One must envisage the possibility of many lives during which, by further transits of consciousness, Essence may receive its vital nourishment. This is a specific interpretation of a much broader idea of great antiquity known as the Theory of Eternal Recurrence, which states that the transits of consciousness at the many levels are circular in character, so that everything is repeated in its own time scale.

Hence it can be suggested that at death one is re-born into the same conditions and repeats the life, possibly more intelligently. The literal mind finds it difficult to comprehend how one can be re-born 'back in time', but we have seen that all the events of life are an illusion of the senses. Since Essence is eternal it is not involved in the cosmic progress of 'clock' time and can provide repeated transits of individual consciousness through the same region.

This is, of course, a theoretical concept which cannot be proved in logical terms, though it does provide a possible explanation of the experience known as déjà vu, the strange feeling of familiarity in certain situations, as if one had been here before. The value of the idea, however, lies in its emotional interpretation, from which one understands that the present life is only part of the pattern. In the full development of Essence it is necessary to contend with all the basic types of experience (represented by the twelve signs of the Zodiac). This progress, though, is only possible when the existing life has been fulfilled.

For this reason it is important *not* to interpret the idea of recurrence in terms of sense-based thinking, which creates the illusion of a mythical 'next time' in which some of the less pleasant experiences may be avoided, or missed opportunities remedied. This is not only imagination, it leads to a complacent belief that there is no urgency. It is the experiences of the *present* life, whatever their character, which have to be utilised *now*, and unless this is done, Essence will not receive the nourishment it requires, so that the experiences will need to be repeated, maybe under less favourable conditions. Indeed, if one accepts the idea at all, the present life is a recurrence of 'last time', so that it is all the more important to take what action is possible now.

* * *

Within the domain of the real world one can envisage the allotted life as a pattern of possibilities which are successively actualised by the transit of consciousness. This constitutes the time-body discussed in Chapter 10, containing all the experiences of the life, including 'future' events which were actualised by the previous recurrence. But as we have seen, this pattern is not rigidly established because individual consciousness can move through the region at different levels.

At the ordinary level of consciousness the transit is mechanical and everything remains the same. A higher level of consciousness, however, can be aware of the pattern as a whole and can arrange a different transit which will permit a more significant use of the possibilities. These are clearly not unrestricted because the pattern has to conform to a variety of associated requirements, such as the conditions of the particular environment, including the lives of many other people, but within these limitations there is a wide range of possibilities which provide the best available opportunities for the nourishment of Essence.

Let us consider briefly what this entails in practical terms. We are allotted a pattern of opportunities (which we do not in general recognise) within which we are permitted to make whatever demands we wish of the Universe. This may sound surprising, but in fact everything that happens to us is the result of a specific demand. This is the law of the Universe which is fundamentally a structure of response to request.

This we do not understand. Our usual prayers are merely wishful thinking, with no recognition of the need for payment. If we find out how to pay, the situation is entirely altered. But in our normal state of sleep we do not even know what demands we are making. We only complain when we do not get our own way.

146

The situation is changed quite magically if we can accept that the events of life are *of our own choosing*, not only in the basic pattern (which we have forgotten) but in its day-to-day implementation. We no longer object to the situations, but regard them as material. We can still pit our wits against the environment, but with a certain lightness of spirit. The feeling of I begins to shift into a more tranquil place, from which one obtains a less personal view of events and their possibilities.

*   *   *

We live by *meaning*. Of the many possibilities available at any moment we select those which provide the greatest sense of purpose. This selection is determined almost entirely by past experience. Our reactions, in fact, are actuated by a continual, but largely unconscious retrospect. However, this can be of two kinds.

Ordinary meaning is concerned with achievement, for which purpose we draw on the experience accumulated in the ordinary memory, which 'cues' the various puppets by which the actions are performed. At the same time, there are other meanings of a different quality which do not involve material considerations but are concerned with ideas of the spirit.

Now in the normal course of existence these different meanings are in conflict. Even material pursuits are not directed by consistent aims, but are subject to a variety of often-changing meanings, in the midst of which we give occasional attention to spiritual ideas when it happens to be convenient. This is not intelligent, for it simply degrades real ideas to the level of material values.

We have seen, however, that a superior level *embraces* the subordinate levels. The emotional levels of the mind can thus provide a different kind of retrospect which is not concerned with achievement but is aware of the experiences in the time-body as a whole, without selection. This exists simultaneously with the ordinary life awareness *which it does not judge*.

This means that as long as this superior awareness is present the necessary activities of life can be undertaken with enjoyment. As St Paul says, "Happy is he that judgeth not himself in that which he approveth". (Rom. 14, 22): and I recall how Dr Nicoll enlivened everything by his sense of delight. A higher level of consciousness does not demand a grim countenance, still less a haughty demeanour.

At the same time, awareness in one's time-body begins to disclose that certain types of experience have served their purpose and need not be continued, even though they still have life meaning. Thus I gave up flying while it was still fun, thereby preserving the experience without nostalgia, but I have other experiences which were continued too long, and turned sour. These can be used, without regrets, as material for transformation by conscious understanding in my time-body.

One has to develop an awareness of what is right at various periods. I remember a dream in which I was on a train journey and got off at a station to buy some papers; but I became involved in a protracted argument over the change, at the end of which the train had left! I mentioned this to Dr Nicoll, who said, "Don't you see; you no longer have need of that kind of money".

Moreover, this greater awareness makes room for many simple activities for which one is all too often 'too busy'. One begins to realise that it is not necessary for everything to show a profit. It is possible to indulge in simple relaxations or artistic pursuits which expect neither reward nor recompense, and which can be savoured without reservation. Such experiences are of more than ordinary value, for anything which is done from genuine delight is a rich source of nourishment which is preserved in the time-body.

* * *

Here surely we are within sight of the Philosopher's Stone, that mystical talisman sought by the ancient alchemists as a connecting link between the material and spiritual worlds. It is becoming evident that this is not a mere allegorical concept, but is an entity having a specific existence in the real world as a kind of lens, which serves to bring into focus the influences from higher levels. Moreover, though we do not normally realise it, this talisman is already in our possession, having been brought with us at birth. It is in discovering how to use it that the task lies.

It is customary at burial services and similar occasions to quote, in heavy tones, the comment of St Paul to Timothy that "we brought nothing into the world, neither can we carry anything out"; but this relates only to physical and psychological possessions, which we have seen to be wholly acquired, and do not belong to us. The real part of a man retains the material of his *transformed* experiences, which serves as equipment for his continuing adventure. He possesses at least a fragment of the magical material of the Philosopher's Stone, which has always seemed to me the great mercy.

However, this magic is of a significantly restricted quality. It is not, and cannot be, concerned with material fortune, for as long as one's feeling of I is entirely absorbed by life situations there can be no alchemy. One is entitled to take a small meed of pleasure from one's successes, for this is a genuine emotion. The puppets who have performed the work are entitled to a brief appreciation, but this must not be prolonged or it will turn sour. Neither must disaster or tragedy be allowed to produce more than transient distress, for these emotions are equally unreal. Yet in practice we prolong all these experiences in the ordinary memory, re-living the successes with nostalgia and the failures with regret.

A different kind of *living* retrospect is required, in which the incidents are recognised, and accepted, as transient aspects of an overall pattern of a much less personal character. This, of course, is by no means easy, for one is inevitably enmeshed in the trammels of ambition, and this makes us very vulnerable. In my own experience I had to suffer the disappoinment of seeing the business on which I had lavished so much care and enthusiasm over the years destroyed by incompetent and insensitive management after my retirement. Yet I was later able to see that this was not only part of the allotted pattern, but was an example of an experience which had served its usefulness.

It is in such conditions that the magic of the Philosopher's Stone can operate. As one begins to withdraw the feeling of I from the realms of personal achievement a different scale of values emerges in which the incidents of life are no more than a part of the real experience. We begin to develop a more consistent meaning within a Universe vastly greater than the confines of our tiny self-importance. Dr Nicoll once said to me "You are much bigger than yourself"—an idea which creates a tremendous sense of release, since it relieves one of the need to keep up the fictitious appearance of oneself.

*   *   *

This is for me a practical philosophy, for by this positive humility I am enabled occasionally to feel myself as an actual part of a Universe of inspiring possibilities; and this creates the understanding that one is not an isolated manifestation but is connected in the real world with other people in the pattern. This idea is expressed in the familiar quotation from John Donne's Devotions—"No man is an Island, entire of itself; every man is a piece of the Continent, a part of the main".

It seems to me that this idea is of much deeper significance than is usually recognised. There are many activities in life which do not fall within one's normal ambit, and it is easy to be envious of other people whose lives appear to attract more exciting or significant experiences. However, we saw in Chapter 11 that people of similar ideals come under the care of a common angel. They are, in fact, all part of a unit (of greater intelligence) in the real world, so that if one can surmount the limitations of individual desire, the real content of the experiences of one's (spiritual) neighbours can indeed be shared.

There is a very important corollary of this idea, which is that I do not have *myself*, to attain the knowledge of the saints in order to achieve understanding. I am continually encountering ideas and interpretations of men of immensely superior understanding, which used to induce feelings of dismay at my inadequacy. Yet if I am in the right (internal) place in myself

I can share these experiences, and rejoice in the illumination which they provide. All I have to do—and all I can do—is to discard the overweening sense of my own importance, and listen to the interpretations of the deeper levels of the mind.

Hence after many excursions I begin to understand the real adventure. It is not concerned with achievement, which is transitory, but with growth of understanding, which is real. By its very nature this is a continuing, and joyous, process which lasts all one's life. One begins to be aware of what Zen Buddhism calls the Totality-which-is-One, so that the necessary duties of life are performed with a kind of impersonal delight. This was very simply expressed by Brother Lawrence, a Carmelite monk of the 17th century, who declared himself to be a very ordinary fellow who tried to do all that was required of him 'in the presence of God'.

INDEX

153

Index

Index

Return journey, 16, 42
Request, 73, 146
Rhine, J. B., 67
Rhythm, 70, 127

Second education, 27
Seed, 49
Self emotions, 64
— love, 63
— remembering, 85
Senses, 22, 30
Sensitivity, 69
Seven, law of, 41, 107, 111
Sex Centre, 54
Sherrington, Sir Charles, 60
Shocks, in octaves, 109
Side Octave, 48, 111, 119
Sleep, 27, 51, 85
Sower, parable of, 49
Space-time continuum, 78
Stimulus, 54
Sun Intelligence, 114, 129
Superspace, 77

Tanha, 50
Time body, 72, 79, 101, 104

— scales, 88
— sense, 91
Three, law of, 40, 92
Transformation, 107, 117, 149
Triad, 40

Understanding, 71
Unity, illusion of, 52, 63
Universe, 39
Unmanifest realms, 16
Upside-down thinking, 38, 77

Vampires, 124
Vis occulta, 81
Vital energy, 120, 131
Voluntary Centres, 53, 85

Westlake, Aubrey, 70
Wisdom of the body, 60, 136
Witnesses, 74
Wonder, sense of, 23
World orders, 40
Wrong psychic functions, 63

Zen Buddhism, 50 151